Learning Together

RONALD G. HELD

GOSPEL PUBLISHING HOUSE
SPRINGFIELD, MISSOURI
02-0571

© 1976 by the Gospel Publishing House, Springfield, Missouri 65802. All rights reserved. This is a Workers Training Division textbook. Credit for its study will be issued under Classification 4, Sunday School Department, Assemblies of God. Library of Congress Catalog Card Number 76-9515. ISBN 0-88243-571-X. Printed in the United States of America.

Contents

1 Jesus the Teacher

Learning is a sharing experience. Students learn from their teacher and from each other. Teachers, too, learn from their students and from each other. That's why we say Sunday school and Christian education are a matter of learning together—learning from each other in discussion and interaction, from the Word in personal study and in group activities. This book seeks to help the teacher bring these many elements together into a teaching/learning experience that is meaningful and fulfilling for everyone involved.

But where do we start in our study of the teaching/learning experience? Do we begin with the teacher or the pupil? Or maybe with an understanding of the teaching/learning process itself? Do we discuss first the lesson plan or the methods employed to carry it out?

And that brings up another question. Where do we go to find a basis, a foundation for our approach to Christian education and Sunday school teaching? There are limitations to what we can get from a secular philosophy of education. Shouldn't Christian education be Biblical in both message and method? Isn't *how* we teach as important as *what* we teach?

Maybe we can find an answer to both questions—where to begin and how to arrive at a Biblical understanding of Christian education—in a study of the greatest Teacher of all. Why not look to the One who made both the teacher and the learner; to the One who both taught the truth and was the Truth.

Jesus is the Christian teacher's example and inspiration. We can best learn to be effective teachers by watching the Master Teacher at work. And the Gospels provide us with just such a record from four different viewpoints. In this opening chapter we want to look at Jesus, the Teacher. We will try to learn what made Him the great teacher He was as we study His attitudes and characteristics as a teacher, and as we analyze the teaching principles He so skillfully employed.

JESUS CAME

Jesus was more than a teacher—much more. He was the Son of God, the Saviour of the world, the Lord of lords. But he *was* a teacher! C. B. Eavey says, "He was often a healer, sometimes a worker of miracles, frequently a preacher, but always a teacher." (C. B. Eavey, *History of Christian Education* [Chicago: Moody Press, 1964], p. 78.) Jesus used teaching as the primary means of conveying the message He came into the world to share. And at the end of His earthly ministry He gave to His followers a teaching commission as the means of continuing what He had begun: "Go ye therefore, and *teach* all nations, baptizing them in the name of the Father, and of the Son, and of the Holy Ghost: *teaching* them to observe all things whatsoever I have commanded you" (Matthew 28:19, 20). In so doing He recognized teaching as essential both to the building of the Kingdom and to the building of Christian character.

Jesus was recognized by all as a great teacher. He referred to himself in this way: "Ye call me Master and Lord: and ye say well; for so I am" (John 13:13). His disciples most often called Him "Master" or "Teacher." Inquirers like Nicodemus and the rich young ruler addressed Him as a teacher. Even His enemies called him, "Teacher." And He is still recognized as a great teacher today. Those who know nothing more about Jesus know He was an outstanding teacher. His methods and His message are studied as classic examples of educational technique.

To us who know Him as Saviour and Lord, He is our Model, our Example, our Pattern. We recognize Him as the Master Teacher par excellence because He perfectly embodied what He taught, He understood His pupils perfectly, and He used perfect methods. He was truly "the way, the truth, and the life" (John 14:6).

Some may question whether the perfection of Christ might tend to discourage those who are far from perfect. "Not so," says Lois LeBar. "Of course, we could never hope to imitate Him, but that isn't what He is asking of us. He is only asking that His strength be made perfect in our weakness. He wants to have such perfect control of us that He is free to work in His own way through us." (Lois LeBar, *Education That Is Christian* [Westwood, NJ: Fleming H. Revell, 1958], p. 51.)

Still others may wonder how Christ's teaching can be compared with our teaching today. After all, He seldom taught in a classroom; we seldom teach outside of one. It is true there is much about the teaching ministry of Christ that was unique because of who He was and when and where He ministered; that could never be duplicated by the human teacher. But there is much that is comparable to teaching today, much that we can follow as a pattern for our teaching. Let's look at some of these together.

THE HEART OF THE TEACHER

Jesus was a great teacher first of all because of how He lived, because of the attitudes that He demonstrated. All that He said was backed up by what He was and what He did. (D. V. Hurst and Dwayne E. Turner, *Mastering the Methods* [Springfield: Gospel Publishing House, 1971], p. 10.)

Love

The most outstanding quality in the life of the Lord was His love—for the world and for the individual. It was love that brought Him into the world and took Him to a cross, but it was also love that made Him effective as a teacher. His heart of love was seen when He was "moved with compassion" toward the multitude (Matthew 9:36); when He looked on the rich young ruler and "beholding him loved him" (Mark 10:21); when He wept at the tomb of His friend, Lazarus (John 11:35).

In the Sermon on the Mount He staked out the boundaries of the law of love that operated in His own life: "Ye have heard that it hath been said, thou shalt love thy neighbor, and hate thine enemy. But I say unto you, love your enemies, bless them that curse you, do good to them that hate you, and pray for them which despitefully use you, and persecute you" (Matthew 5:43, 44). In other words it was an *unconditional* love—a love that reaches both the lovely and the unlovely. And He practiced what He preached. He not only took little children in His arms and blessed them, but He looked on His tormentors from the cross and prayed, "Father, forgive them."

Jesus not only sat on a mountain and talked about love, He also walked the dusty roads of His world and ministered love by reaching, by touching, by giving of himself. He was not content to give a discourse about love, as some are today. He put His love into *action*. And one day He climbed another mountain and let love nail Him to a cross. He knew what it meant to say, "Greater love hath no man than this, that a man lay down his life for his friends" (John 15:13). No wonder He made love the identifying mark of His followers.

Excitement

Jesus was an enthusiastic person. There was a vibrancy and an air of excitement that surrounded Him. Can you imagine the excitement when He made a whip and drove the moneychangers out of the temple? Or when He stood up at the last day of the feast and cried, "If any man thirst, let him come unto me, and drink" (John 7:37)?

Control

At the same time He demonstrated a poise that revealed that He was in control of every situation. In the midst of a storm, He could sleep. During the height of His popularity, when the multitude would have taken Him by force and made Him their King, He slipped quietly away. Before the Sanhedrin, Pilate, and Herod He stood with dignity. "Poised intensity" may be a good phrase to describe this combination of excitement and self-control that He exhibited.

Approachableness

People felt free to come to Jesus with their questions, their problems, their personal needs. They responded to His invitation: "Come unto me, all ye that labor and are heavy laden" (Matthew 11:28). One half of the teaching incidents in the Gospels were initiated by the learners themselves. Some, like Nicodemus, came to find answers to questions that were bothering them. Others, like Jairus, came to seek His help in a time of personal tragedy. They came knowing they would find a sympathetic, understanding listener; One who would not turn them away, One who would help them unravel life's mysteries, One who would act on their behalf. And as they came, He taught them about himself, about themselves, and about the kingdom of heaven.

Optimism

Jesus had faith in people. He saw potential where others saw only problems. This can be seen in His choice of disciples. Most of them would have been prime candidates for selection as "those most unlikely to succeed." But Jesus knew that Peter, the impetuous, flamboyant fisherman, had potential to become the preacher of Pentecost. In John, one of the "sons of thunder," He saw a tenderness that would make him the disciple of love.

And Jesus was patient enough to let these potentials develop. He believed in the growth and development of the spiritual nature of the learner. He said, "First the blade, then the ear, after that the full corn in the ear" (Mark 4:28). With the disciples the process at times seemed slow, almost hopeless. But eventually His investment in time and teaching paid off. And then He took the greatest risk of all—He left the work of preaching the gospel in the hands of His disciples.

Communion

Jesus lived in close communion with His Heavenly Father. No one can study the life of the Master without being aware of the great emphasis He placed on prayer. After a day of ministry, during which He had healed many people, Jesus rose up "a great while before day" and went out to pray (Mark 1:35). Before He chose His 12 disciples He spent the night in prayer (Luke 6:12). In the hour of agony in the Garden He prayed (Mark 14:35, 36). The prayer life of Jesus was so impressive that His disciples came to Him requesting, "Lord, teach us to pray" (Luke 11:1). Much of the prayer concern of Jesus was for others, very often it was for those He was teaching. The entire 17th chapter of John is a prayer of Christ for His disciples and for those who would come after them.

Jesus was in the habit of attending services in the synagogue and temple: "And as his custom was, he went into the synagogue on the sabbath day" (Luke 4:16). He also had the highest regard for the Word of God, the Old Testament Scriptures (Matthew 5:18, 19). And He knew the Word. As he walked with the two disciples on the road to Emmaus, "beginning at Moses and all the prophets, he expounded unto them in all the scriptures the things concerning himself" (Luke 24:27).

In these and many other ways Jesus showed us what it means to have the heart of a teacher.

CHARACTERISTICS OF HIS TEACHING

1. *Emphasis on the Pupil*

Jesus knew the worth of the individual and made him the focal point of His teaching. Paul Lowenberg has said, "While Jesus Christ preached to tremendous audiences, yet He never forgot the value of an individual soul. Again and again and again the King of kings and Lord of lords turned His attention to individuals. These were the objects of His search and of His love." *(Our Mission in Today's World* [Springfield: Gospel Publishing House, 1968], p. 22.) And the Gospels bear this out: we read of one Nicodemus, one woman at the well, one man born blind, one Lazarus, one Bartimaeus, one Zacchaeus.

Jesus also recognized the individual differences in His students. Each learner was different, each need different. For example, think of the diversity among His disciples —fishermen, tax collector, zealot. In a sense He graded His teaching to fit the characteristics, experience, and background of His pupils. The way He dealt with Nicodemus in John 3, for instance, was far different from the way He dealt with the woman at the well in John 4.

And Jesus did not expect the same response from each pupil. Notice this emphasis in several of His parables. In the parable of the seed and the soil even the good ground yielded a diverse harvest: "Some thirty, and some sixty, and some an hundred" (Mark 4:8). In the Parable of the Talents the householder gave to one five talents, to another two, and to another one (Matthew 25:14). And each was responsible only for what he had been given.

Findley Edge points out another interesting feature of the educational ministry of Jesus—the freedom which He allowed His learners. "He left the individual free to think for himself and to choose for himself." (Findley B. Edge, *Teaching for Results* [Nashville: Broadman Press, 1956], p. 8.) This was in sharp contrast to the thinking of His contemporaries who demanded strict adherence to Jewish laws and traditions with little room for individual initiative.

2. Informal Teaching

Two words that are very descriptive of the teaching style of Christ are *walked* and *talked*. Eavey says, "As He moved among people, it was His habit to talk in a natural, friendly and intimate way of the things pertaining to the kingdom of God." (Eavey, *op. cit.*, p. 79.) He could be found teaching by the wayside, on the seashore, in a desert place, on a mountain, in a home, by a well, in the temple court or synagogue. He went where the people were, observing them in their daily living, concerning himself with their needs. He taught in a very natural, conversational manner, using informal methods such as questions and answers, dialogue, storytelling, and so on.

3. Profound Simplicity

One of the unique characteristics of Jesus' teaching was His ability to teach profound truth in a simple manner. This was because He talked to people in a language they could understand. He drew upon the experiences and environment of His hearers. His teaching was a part of life, not apart from life. His listeners knew what He was talking about and could easily understand the great lessons He taught by parable and story. He related seed to the kingdom of God, wind and water to the Spirit, sheep and goats to the day of judgment, the lost sheep to the love of God. No wonder "the common people heard him gladly" (Mark 12:37).

4. Authority

A multitude of people returned from hearing the Sermon on the Mount astonished, "For He taught them as one having authority, and not as the scribes" (Matthew 7:28, 29). Those in Capernaum who heard Him teach on the Sabbath days, too, were astonished, "For his word was with power" (Luke 4:32). A band of officers sent out by the chief priests to take Him into custody returned empty-handed. Their only excuse for disobeying orders: "Never man spake like this man" (John 7:46).

These incidents all attest to the authority with which Jesus taught. What a contrast to the traditional educational approach of His contemporaries. The teaching formula of the scribes, who appealed to ancient authorities to be accepted and believed, went something like this: "Rabbi A says that Rabbi B says . . ." or "Rabbi C says in the name of Rabbi

D . . ." (Edge, *op. cit.*, p. 3.) Jesus dared to say, "Ye have heard that it was said by them of old time . . . but I say unto you . . ." (Matthew 5:21, 22). The authority of the scribes was external, secondhand; His authority was internal, fresh, and free.

What was the source of His authority? Jesus credited His authority as coming from the divine commission of His Heavenly Father. "All authority hath been given unto me in heaven and on earth" (Matthew 28:18, ASV). In part, His authority came from His penetrating insights into the meaning and message of the Old Testament Scriptures. Certainly a part of it was found in the life He lived. It could be summed up by saying His credentials were himself—*who* He was, *what* He taught, and *how* He taught.

TEACHING PRINCIPLES OF JESUS

Jesus was successful as a teacher because He based His teaching on certain important principles of teaching and learning. He understood the human mind and adapted His teaching approaches to agree with the way in which the pupil learned.

He Taught With a Definite Aim

Jesus never taught merely for the sake of teaching. He always had a purpose in mind. Jesus' central aim in teaching was to communicate a new life and relationship to God. He said, "I am come that they might have life, and that they might have it more abundantly" (John 10:10). Upon this new relationship He sought to develop new insights and proper attitudes. He further sought to prepare the learner to effectively meet life's problems, to grow toward maturity, and to train for service. This new life was to be the result of two things: a spiritual *new birth* and spiritual *growth*.

The teaching aims of Christ were focused on a response on the part of the learner. Eavey says, "He was not so much concerned with imparting knowledge as He was with stimulating to action in terms of what was already known."

(Eavey, *op. cit.*, p. 79.) To Him there was something far more important than for the person merely to know truth. He desired above all else that the learner see the bearing the truth had upon every phase of his life and begin to put the truth into practice in his living. He stressed this concept in His teaching when He said, "By their fruits ye shall know them" (Matthew 7:20). And, "If ye know these things, happy are ye if ye do them" (John 13:17).

Though Jesus did not teach from a written curriculum, there is definite evidence of order in His teaching and progression toward His objectives. A careful look at the content of His teaching will reveal that He often grouped the learning experiences of His pupils around a central theme. See for example the series of parables in Mark 4 on the internal nature of the Kingdom. Or the rapid-fire succession of miracles in chapters 4 and 5—calming the storm at sea, delivering the Gadarene demoniac, healing the woman with the issue of blood, raising Jairus' daughter—all to prove His complete mastery over every realm—natural, demonic, physical, even death.

He also graded His teaching to fit the capabilities of His learners. An example of this is His teaching the disciples of His coming death on the cross. He alluded briefly to the fact early in His ministry, but did not begin to teach directly on the subject until near the end of His earthly ministry—after He had been with His disciples for nearly 3 years. And even then He waited until the setting was just right (Matthew 16:13-21).

He Started With Pupils' Needs

The way in which Jesus taught the woman at the well in John 4 is an excellent example of His approach to pupils' needs. As the woman approached the well where Jesus was sitting, He asked her for a drink. In that simple request He accomplished several important things: He aroused curiosity and questions, He aroused interest in Him as a Person, and He gave opportunity for active response. (LeBar, *op. cit.,*

p. 53.) She came to draw water; so that's where He started, beginning with her felt need—physical water—but He did not leave her there. He went on to lead her to her real need—living water. From this point of contact He brought her to a knowledge of himself as the Messiah. Within moments she was returning to the city saying, "Come, see a man who told me all that I ever did. Can this be the Christ?" (John 4:29, RSV).

This approach was typical. Jesus centered His teaching around life situations with the purpose of meeting deep personal needs. He began with the person where he was in his experience. From there He turned to the Word of God for help in meeting that need and then back to the learner for the application of that truth in life. We could apply the words of Christ in John 14:6 to this pattern and diagram it in this way:

He Emphasized Learning-by-Doing

Jesus knew that the pupil must learn to think and act for himself. And so He sought to involve his students in the learning process. He sent out the Twelve and the Seventy to preach and heal. It was the disciples who distributed the bread and fish to the multitude and saw it multiply in their hands. They were the ones who rolled away the stone from the tomb of Lazarus. The four men who brought their friend to Jesus had to remove a section of the roof to get him in. It was Peter who walked on the water, and who caught a fish with a coin in its mouth. In each case there was pupil participation. The principle of learning-by-doing was in operation. His teaching itself was filled with words of action: "come," "go," "follow," "do."

Sometimes the action was less direct, but it was real just the same. Jesus often used questions to get His learners personally involved in the teaching situation and to lead them into the truth. He often answered a question with a question to make the learner think for himself. (LeBar, *op. cit.* pp. 83, 84.)

He Taught With Variety

Jesus was a master in the use of teaching methods. Some of those he used were:

1. *Questions.* A great share of Jesus' teaching was composed of questions and answers. Well over 100 of His questions are recorded. It would make an interesting study to compile a list of these questions. You would find that Jesus used questions to introduce a story, to emphasize a truth, to arouse curiosity, to recall information, to express emotions, to probe motives, to silence His accusers, to express a need, to prepare the mind of the listener, to clarify thinking, to determine understanding, to relate His message to life, and to secure personal lesson response.

Most of the questions Jesus asked did not call for the repetition of mere factual knowledge, but were provocative questions calling for a thoughtful, personal reply. For example: "Whom do men say that I am?" "But whom say ye that I am?" (Mark 8:27, 29). Several times Jesus used a rhetorical question such as: "For what is a man profited, if he shall gain the whole world, and lose his own soul? or what shall a man give in exchange for his soul?" (Matthew 16:26).

2. *Discussion.* The discussion method used by Jesus was more of a conversational type of discussion. It usually involved Him and one other person in dialogue. Some of the

most significant, most oft-quoted words of Jesus come from these personal conversations. For example, it was to Nicodemus that He said, "Except a man be born again, he cannot see the kingdom of God" (John 3:3). And, "For God so loved the world, that he gave his only begotten Son, that whosoever believeth in him should not perish, but have everlasting life" (John 3:16). And to a sinful Samaritan woman He revealed the nature of God and the mode of spiritual worship: "God is a Spirit: and they that worship him must worship him in spirit and in truth" (John 4:24).

3. *Lecture.* Jesus was a skillful speaker. His listeners, in small groups and large, were captivated by His words. There are some 60 discourses of Jesus recorded in the Gospels, some as short as a few well-chosen statements, others as long as four chapters in John. The settings varied from formal—the synagogue—to informal—mountainside or seashore.

The lectures of Jesus are characterized by their relevance to the real-life needs of His listeners. Often He anticipated the questions of His listeners and incorporated them into His messages. The Christian teacher would do well to study some of the most prominent of Christ's discourses such as the Sermon on the Mount, or His farewell message in John 14-17, as examples of effective use of the lecture method.

4. *Stories.* Jesus was unquestionably the world's greatest storyteller. This method stands out from all the others and was used by Jesus more than any of the others. He talked about plants and animals and aspects of everyday life. But most often He told stories about people. Over half of the recorded stories of Jesus had to do with people.

Jesus' purposes in using stories and parables were: to stimulate thought, to create a lasting impression, to win and hold attention, and to relate new truth to old. Lois LeBar suggests that Jesus used parables because they could be comprehended by each listener according to his own spiritual capacity. Someone with little or no interest in spiritual things could walk away without further rejecting the truth and hardening his heart. While a genuine seeker could understand in part and inquire further if he wanted to. (LeBar, *op. cit.*, pp. 69, 70.)

The teacher could learn much about the art of storytelling by studying some of Jesus' classic stories such as the Lost Sheep, the Good Samaritan, the Ten Virgins, and so forth.

5. *Teaching aids.* Jesus made effective use of the teaching aids He had at His disposal. He used *illustrations* from nature, from current events, from life around Him. He set a child in the midst of His disciples to illustrate what would be required of them to enter the kingdom of heaven. He used *objects* and demonstrations. By washing His disciples' feet, Jesus demonstrated humility.

Someone has suggested that Jesus had the biggest and best flannelboard of all. He had the Sea of Galilee for a background, a stony path for a foreground, and His figures were real-life people who came and went at His will.

D. V. Hurst quoting C. F. McCoy says: "Although Jesus only taught for about three years, yet after nineteen hundred years, He still stands as the supreme example for the Christian teacher. He still teaches today. In His life, message, and method He still serves as our *goal*, our *model*, and our *criterion*. He presents an inexhaustible study, a boundless source of instruction and inspiration." (D. V. Hurst, *And He Gave Teachers* [Springfield: Gospel Publishing House, 1955], p. 90.)

In the rest of this book, we will explore further many of the principles introduced in this opening chapter.

2 A Matter of Relationships

What do you remember most about your early experiences in Sunday school, or any institution of learning for that matter? Was it the place—the buildings, the rooms? Was it the organization with leaders serving in various capacities? Or maybe the activities—the things you did in Sunday school? Do you recall much about the specific content of the lessons?

You undoubtedly have memories of all of these aspects of Sunday school; but if you're like most, you probably remember more about the people in Sunday school than anything else—the teachers you had, the pupils you associated with. That's because learning is often more a matter of relationships than structure, activities, facilities, or even subject matter. We remember more about *who* taught us than we do about *what* they taught.

The same is true of the Sunday school. As important as the subject matter is, it is probably not what leaves the greatest impression. Rather it is the quality of the interpersonal relationships. Sunday school, when you reduce the definition to its simplest terms, is what happens between the teacher and the pupils in the classroom. It is a teacher and pupils gathered around the Word, finding answers to their life-needs together. It's a matter of person-to-person and Person-to-person relationships, for the Living Word is there in the person of the Holy Spirit.

In this chapter we want to look at the two main principals in the classroom—the teacher and the pupil—and their relationship with each other.

FOCUS ON THE TEACHER

How would you describe a real Christian teacher? Well, maybe we just did! A real Christian teacher is a *Christian,* a *real person,* and a *teacher.* Let's look at each of these elements.

First and foremost, a teacher must be a CHRISTIAN, and not just a person who calls himself a Christian or who had a conversion experience once many years ago. He must be a true follower of Christ, have an up-to-date experience with Christ, and be growing in his relationship with the Lord.

Of course, there are other marks of a Christian as well. He is filled with the power of the Holy Spirit. He is a student of the Word, and not just as it relates to the lesson from week to week. He has a consistent prayer life. He is a careful steward of his time, his resources, his abilities. He is faithful to the local church and its leaders. He effectively shares his faith with others. He is guided by Christian principles in private as well as in public, at home as well as at church. And the list could go on and on.

A real Christian teacher is also a REAL PERSON. What do we mean by a "real person"? Someone who is genuine, an honest person, someone who is not a phony. These are terms that might be used. A real person is authentic. He tries to avoid pretense. He is what he appears to be. He is honest, both with God and with his class. As Allan Hart Jahsman put it: "A real teacher becomes a model to learners—not a plastic cast saint, but someone who shares his own feelings of inadequacy and his reliance on the adequacy that comes from Christ." ("A Real Christian Teacher," *Interaction,* Sept. 1974, p. 13.)

This raises an interesting point: You don't have to be perfect to be an effective teacher. Your students are very aware of your humanity. They're waiting for you to admit the fact and be open and honest with them.

Now it is possible to go to extremes in this area. But at the same time your students need to see that you are a fellow traveler—that you haven't yet quite arrived, but that you're working at it—and that you want to share some of the things you've learned along the way that may help them.

And don't be afraid to accept help from them either. The roles of student and teacher can sometimes be reversed in the classroom to the mutual benefit of all. What teacher has not marveled at the insights into Scripture that have been shared with the class by one of the students?

There is something else involved in being a real person, and that is to accept people as they are, for what they are. A real Christian teacher respects his students, young or old, as real people. This means he tries to put himself in his students' place. He tries to see things from their viewpoint. He respects their opinions and ideas. He works hard at creating a warm atmosphere and good communication in his class with his students. He has learned to be a good listener as well as a good talker. He spends time with his students away from the church and classroom. He is available, but not "pushy." He laughs with them, cries with them, plays with them, and prays with them. In a word—he LOVES them.

And then, of course, a real Christian teacher is a **TEACHER.** He knows how to function in the classroom —preparing challenging lessons, directing meaningful learning activities, bringing his students to a point of decision and commitment to the lesson truth. He has a thorough grasp of his subject and its related materials. He has some basic skills in the use of teaching methods. He is constantly working to improve those skills through reading, attendance at staff meetings, and participation in training programs, seminars, conventions, and so on.

MOTIVES FOR TEACHING

Another factor that enters into the teacher-pupil relationship is motive. Have you ever asked yourself, "Why am I a Sunday school teacher?" Larry Richards explores this area in his book, *You the Teacher.* (Chicago: Moody Press, pp. 49, 50.) He points out that some teach out of a sense of responsibility. They know how difficult it is for the Sunday school to enlist enough teachers and so they dutifully shoulder their share of the responsibility.

Another may teach out of friendship or obligation to someone in the church, maybe the pastor or one of the Sunday school officers. Others serve because they got started years ago, and there doesn't seem to be any graceful way to quit or anyone to take their place. Besides, everyone just expects them to keep at it till Jesus comes. Still others may be teachers because they like that pat on the back, the fact that the pastor and others look up to them or feel they are "good Christians" because of what they do for the Lord.

A sense of responsibility, an expression of friendship, habit, a desire to be looked up to—so many motives for teaching. Some of them are acceptable up to a point, but not really adequate for the teacher who wants to develop the best of relationships with his students.

A true Christian teacher has a higher motive for teaching. He serves out of a deep feeling of love for Christ and a desire to please Him. He teaches because he cares about his students and wants to help them grow in their Christian experience toward maturity in Christ. He knows that if his heart is not really in what he is doing or if his motives are not right, his students will sense this and not relate to him as they should.

PATTERNS OF RELATIONSHIP

How you view your students will greatly affect the kind of personal relationship you establish in your class. In view of this, it might be helpful to define some of the different teacher-pupil patterns and the responses each creates.

The *authoritarian* teacher feels that he alone can satisfactorily direct the learning activities of the class. He believes he must exercise firm control of the class and expects the students to explicitly obey his directions. He is the final authority figure in the classroom, so he must have the answers to any questions, and his students must accept his answers. (Lawrence O. Richards, *Creative Bible Teaching*

[Chicago: Moody Press, 1970], p. 131.) In this relationship the teacher, then, is central.

The result of this relationship, as you might imagine, is pupil apathy and resentment. If differing opinions are not welcome, they will soon no longer be offered. Attendance often declines. Students who do remain under the influence of this kind of teaching become dependent and unresourceful.

The *free-reign* teacher tends to let the students decide what they want to do and how they will do it. He really doesn't lead at all, but depends on each student to set his own course of action and study determined by his personal initiative and interest. Here the student is central.

Strangely enough, the result of this relationship is also pupil apathy. Teaching aims are not clearly defined, discussions reach no conclusions, plans and decisions are not followed up with action. The students tend to be insecure; they are never quite sure where they stand.

The *democratic* teacher shares responsibility for planning and participating in class activities with his students. He is interested in stimulating the students to become involved in meaningful Bible study for themselves. In this kind of relationship there is mutual give and take.

The result of this kind of relationship, obviously, is pupil development and initiative. Decisions are made by the group and acted upon by them. Each student knows he has the support and personal concern of his teacher.

What kind of teacher-pupil relationship will you establish? Will you do all the talking and rely on the power of your office to get your students to sit and listen? Or will you get them personally involved in the learning process? Will you sit back and let the class make its own way? Or will you help the class crystallize its thinking and set a course of action together?

Do you see yourself as a boss or as a friend? If you are a friend, you have no reputation to uphold, no rights to defend. Your students don't need a boss, but they could use a friend.

FOCUS ON THE PUPIL

The pupil is central in Christian education; all activities focus on him. The teaching process begins where he is, on his level with his interests and needs. The Bible is made relevant to the pupil and becomes a part of his life by means of the teaching ministry of the human teacher working in cooperation with the Holy Spirit.

A Biblical View of the Pupil

Several assumptions about the pupil become obvious from a study of the Biblical view of man. The Bible teaches that man is created in the image of God (Genesis 1:26). As such, he possesses much potential for development. But he is also a sinner, separated from His Creator, and in need of salvation (Romans 3:23). It is at this point that the Christian educator differs from the secular humanist who has high admiration for human achievement and the goodness of man. The Christian teacher seeks to provide opportunity for each pupil to come into a genuine personal experience with God through faith in the redemptive work of Christ (Romans 5:1). After experiencing salvation, the pupil must be guided toward maturity in Christ (Ephesians 4:13, 15). The Christian teacher must remember that his pupils, like himself, have not yet arrived, but are in the process of becoming; they are growing toward maturity.

Individual Differences

Students come in all shapes, sizes, and descriptions. There are great differences in their rate of physical, mental, emotional, social, and spiritual growth. Every teacher knows that students with approximately the same formal training can be quite different from each other. Some are very adept in dealing with ideas, while others have great mechanical or mathematical ability. This is further complicated by the fact that pupils come into Sunday school with great differences in Biblical knowledge and spiritual development. The effective teacher will strive to deal with individuals as much as possible. He will realize that he is not teaching a class, but pupils; not a group, but individuals.

GETTING TO KNOW THE PUPIL

If the pupil is so important, it is necessary that the Christian teacher know more about him as a person. Bible teaching must be as closely related to the needs of the pupils as possible. The more the teacher knows about his pupil, the more effective he will be in teaching him.

What Should You Know About the Pupil?

Family. You should know the size of the pupil's family. Knowing whether he is an only child or one of a large number of children may explain certain behavioral problems. How is the child disciplined at home? You should know something about the socioeconomic status of the family. Does the pupil have everything he wants or does he come from a deprived family? Is it a happy home or is it a broken home? What kind of relationship does the pupil have with his parents, or the parents with their children? Does the home provide supplemental Christian training? Can you call on the parents to help the pupil study his lesson or learn a memory verse?

Church. You should know something about the pupil's church background and that of his family. Is he a member of the church? For how long? Does he attend regularly? What is his doctrinal background? What other church activities is the pupil involved in? You should also know if the pupil's close friends are from church or outside.

Spiritual experiences. You should definitely know whether the pupil has accepted Christ as his Saviour, and if he is growing in his Christian experience. Has the pupil been baptized in water? Has he received the baptism in the Holy Spirit? Has he established personal habits of Bible reading and prayer? Is he sharing his faith with others? It may help in lesson preparation if you know some of the spiritual problems of your pupils.

School. You should know what grade the pupil is in and, with younger children, who his teacher is. If the pupil has difficulty understanding the material in the lesson or seems unchallenged by it, the explanation may lie in knowing how he is doing in his studies at school. With teens you should know what extracurricular activities they are involved in. Are they active in sports? Is someone from your class on the team? With adults it will help to know their educational background. What degrees, if any, do they hold? What special training do they have? Are they involved in any program of continuing education?

Job. You should know what vocational interests your teenagers have. Do they have jobs now? With adults it will be helpful to know where they work, how long they have had the same job, what their hours are, and what special skills they need to do their job. You also should know if they are happy with their work. Retirees can be used in the church if you know what they used to do on the job.

Personal. You should know your pupils' birthdays and ages. Something as simple as knowing if they have a nickname may be important. You and his grandmother may be the only two people in the world who call him "Theodore"—his family and all his friends call him "Skip." You should know what their hobbies and other interests are and what they do with their leisure time. Are they involved in community activities? What leadership qualities do they possess?

How Can You Find Out This Information?

Personal questionnaire. A personal questionnaire can be used to gather much factual information such as birthday, age, size of family, church membership, school grade, extracurricular activities, educational background, job, and so on.

Visit. Some of the more subjective information can only be gotten by visiting the pupil in his home or neighborhood, at school or on the job. Plan to visit each pupil at least once or twice a year. A visit to the pupil's schoolteacher might prove helpful and will also show that your Sunday school takes a personal interest in each pupil as does the public school.

Observation. A good deal of information can be discovered by the teacher who is observant of his pupils in casual, informal settings outside of the classroom. Be alert to opportunities to observe your pupils at other church services and activities, in their home and neighborhood, in chance meetings in public, etc. The information gained from these observations may be more accurate than that gotten in other ways.

Conferences. With teens and adults it may be helpful to schedule a conference with each pupil sometime at the beginning of the new Sunday school year. Such conferences will give opportunity to engage the pupil in conversation, determine his spiritual progress and real needs, and counsel with him.

How Can You Use This Information?

The information you gather must be arranged in some usable form. One idea would be to compile a notebook with a page or two for each pupil in your class. These pages could contain factual data about the pupil, your impressions about him, a running commentary about his spiritual development, interesting anecdotes from class experiences, and so on. This information should be kept somewhat confidential. When the pupil is promoted, this information should be passed on to the next teacher.

Pupil information can be most helpful in planning the lessons to meet real needs, in tapping the personal interests of your pupils, and in helping to solve personal problems. This notebook should be consulted as you prepare your lesson and as you pray for your pupils. You will also want to consult this notebook before you visit the pupil or his family. Relating an interesting experience about the pupil from class may help to begin a conversation with the parents.

As you will see in chapter 9, some of this information is also helpful in evaluating your pupils and your teaching.

The class period has ended and most of the pupils have left the room—except Jeremy. He's hoping for a chance to talk to his teacher about a need in his life. The teacher, however, is in a hurry and leaves the room with a quick "See you."

A less determined student would have dropped it right there, but not Jeremy. He's got a problem and he's got to talk to somebody! He finally catches up with the teacher in the hall.

"Mr. Myer, can I talk with you a minute?"

"Oh sure, sure, Jeremy," he says as people pass by on both sides on their way to the worship service. "What can I do for you?"

"Well, some of the kids at school are planning a pot party after the game Saturday night, and I'm wondering. . . ."

"Yes, I see what you mean. Why, when I was your age, I faced the same problem. Just had to work it out for myself. Oh, hello, Fred. Be there in a minute," says the teacher as he glances at his watch.

"But you see, I was planning to go to the game with them and now. . . ."

" 'Shun the very appearance of evil.' That's what the Bible says. I think if you'd just read the Bible more, you'd know the right thing to do. Got to go now."

Jeremy turns away, and his teacher hurries off to meet his friend, "Fred, you wouldn't believe what that Harris boy just told me. There's going to be a pot party Saturday, and he's. . . ."

You don't have to be a professional counselor to know that this teacher broke just about every rule in the counselor's handbook. He was in too much of a hurry. There was no privacy. The teacher did most of the talking. He lapsed into a recitation of ancient history and gave overly simplistic answers to the student's problem. And worst of all, he did not keep confidences.

Qualities of a Good Counseling Teacher

By contrast then, what are the marks of an effective counseling teacher?

1. A good counselor must be trustworthy and able to keep confidences. As someone has said, "He must have a heart like a graveyard—many problems will lie buried there." The teacher must resist the temptation to use actual situations learned in personal counseling as lesson illustrations, even when he thinks "the names have been changed to protect the innocent."

2. The counselor must be available and willing to take time to help. But he must also avoid the opposite danger of throwing himself at, or forcing himself on, his pupils.

3. A good counselor must be a good listener. It is impossible to listen if you are doing all the talking. Instead ask questions that will help to clarify issues. And try not to be shocked by what you may hear.

4. A good counseling teacher must show genuine love and compassion for others and demonstrate an understanding and patient attitude. Pupils, young and old alike, will recognize the real thing when they see it. Let them know you understand how they feel, but avoid becoming too emotionally involved with their problems.

5. A good counselor should be alert to evidences of a desire for help. Pupils in need of counseling will not always seek that help. Cultivate a "sixth sense" to detect that need; and if necessary, initiate the counseling situation yourself.

6. The counseling teacher must evidence spiritual depth and maturity that will inspire confidence in his pupils. His own life must be firmly rooted in the Word of God. He must demonstrate stability and emotional maturity in his personal life.

7. A good counselor will not preach to his pupils or recite ancient history dating back to the time "when I was your age." He will avoid trying to apply personal solutions to other people's problems, or making decisions for the pupil that he should make for himself.

8. A good counselor will learn to use the Bible wisely in his counseling. He will not hesitate to show what the Bible says concerning the matter, but he will not offer overly simplistic answers to complicated problems.

Counseling Opportunities

Some of the ideas discussed in the section above regarding getting to know the pupil—observation, visits, conferences—can also serve as counseling opportunities. Other opportunities are:

Before and after class. It is extremely important that the teacher be in the classroom when the pupils begin to arrive. Also be alert to pupils who may linger in the room after the class is dismissed.

Other church activities. Prayer times around the altar provide excellent opportunities to counsel and pray with your students. This means you must be present at all the church services.

Casual meetings outside of church. Go where your pupils are: in their neighborhood, at school activities, at work. Take time to visit briefly with your pupils wherever you run into them. Be friendly and open with them.

3 Understand Teaching and Learning

What is your understanding of your role as a teacher? What do you know about the way in which your pupils learn? Maybe the first question we need to settle is: "Why do we need to understand the teaching/learning process in the first place?"

A Christian teacher need not have a degree in educational psychology to be an effective communicator of God's Word. But a basic understanding of how the pupil learns and the role of the teacher in the classroom can be very helpful. The teaching staff of the Sunday school should work from the same basic teaching/learning philosophy. An understanding of how your pupils learn will help you evaluate their progress and assist those who are having difficulties. Understanding your role as a teacher will determine how you plan your lessons, what methods you use, how you structure the learning environment, and so on.

A LOOK AT LEARNING

Henrietta Mears said: "The teacher has not taught until the pupil has learned." So before you can understand your role as a teacher, you must understand how the pupil learns. If you are going to teach effectively, you must teach in accordance with the ways in which the pupil learns.

What Others Have Said

In her book, *Learning Is Change*, Martha Leypoldt defines the learning process in terms of change. (Valley Forge: Judson Press, 1971, pp. 31-33.) She speaks of cognitive learning, or change in knowledge; affective learning, or change in attitudes; and psychomotor learning, or change in conduct. Learning is change that affects *knowing, feeling,* and *doing.* The pupil has not learned until his head, heart, and life are changed by what he has learned.

The pupil can learn at several different levels. Lawrence O. Richards identifies five levels that are important for the Christian teacher in his book, *Creative Bible Teaching.* (Chicago: Moody Press, 1968, pp. 69-73.)

Rote learning—the ability to repeat something from memory without thought of the meaning, such as repeating Scripture verses from memory.

Recognition—the ability to recognize and understand the meaning of Biblical concepts.

Restatement—the ability to think through the meaning of Biblical truths and express them in one's own words.

Relation—the ability to relate Biblical truths to life, to see ways in which Biblical truths can be practiced in specific situations in life.

Realization—the ability to make Biblical truth real in experience by applying it in daily life.

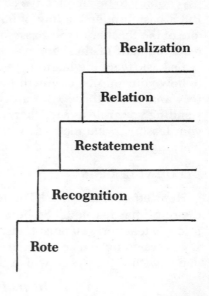

To be able to repeat a Biblical concept from rote memory is not enough. Neither is the ability to recognize a Biblical concept and understand its meaning. Even the ability to express a Biblical concept in one's own words and to see its implications for life stops short of the goal of real learning. The goal of the Christian teacher is to guide his pupils to personally respond to a Biblical truth and begin to act upon it and apply it in their lives.

Lois LeBar defines effective learning as an "inner, active, continuous, disciplined process under the authority of the Word of God and the control of the Holy Spirit in the direction of maturity in Christ." (LeBar, *op. cit.*, pp. 167, 168.) It is an inner process in the sense that growth takes place in the pupils' inner lives through the meeting of their needs. Learning is an active process in that the pupils are participating, interacting, and discovering God's truths for themselves. Learning is continuous in that it is a steady on-going process, proceeding from the known to the unknown. And learning is a disciplined process in that there is guidance, control, and authority in the teaching/learning process.

How the Pupil Learns

Several basic principles are important to an understanding of how the pupil learns:

1. *The pupil learns best when he is ready to learn.*

The learning process must start with the pupil where he is—with his needs and interests. He must be prepared to receive Biblical truth by looking for answers to a question or solutions to a problem. This means the teacher must first gain his students' interest and arouse their curiosity. He must start with their felt needs and lead to their real needs.

Another principle of learning involved here is that the pupil learns by proceeding from the known to the unknown. This means the teacher must know where his pupils are in their knowledge and understanding of, and their response to, spiritual truth. He must also grade his teaching to the learning capabilities of his students at their particular stage of mental and spiritual development.

The pupil will also learn more readily when he can see the

relationship of the parts to the whole. So it may be necessary, then, for the teacher to preview a new series of lessons with his students and keep past lessons in focus by periodic review.

2. *The pupil learns through his senses.*

Learning is a "sensorial" experience. The student has only one way to learn and that is through his five senses—the gateways to his mind. These commonly accepted figures point this out:

Pupils' Ability to Retain Information

up to 10% of what they hear
up to 30% of what they see
up to 50% of what they see and hear
up to 70% of what they see, hear, and say
up to 90% of what they see, hear, say, and do

Method of Teaching	Recall 3 Hours	Recall 3 Days
Telling alone	70%	10%
Showing alone	72%	20%
Telling & showing	85%	65%

The most effective teaching methods and aids, then, are those which involve a combination of the senses. This fact has implications for using a variety of methods and teaching aids.

3. *The pupil learns through activity.*

This is the most important principle concerning the way in which the pupil learns. Learning is not a *passive* experience; it is an *active* process. It is not something that *happens* to the pupil; it is something he *does*. The difference between these two concepts—active and passive learning—is the difference between the spectator in the stands and the athlete out on the field or court. One is only looking on; the other is actively involved.

Have you noticed that you as the teacher seem to get more

from your lessons than your students at times? This is because you are actively involved in studying and preparing your lessons. Your pupils must be involved in the same process of Bible study. They need to do their own investigation, to use research materials, to discover the meaning of the passage, to find answers to their problems, to come to personal decisions. The secret of good teaching is to try to involve the pupils in the same process of study you engaged in as the teacher.

The charts on page 34 and the diagram on page 36 point out that the greater the level of activity and involvement, the more effective the learning will be.

4. *The pupil learns best when he is motivated to learn.*

He will learn most rapidly when learning is made desirable and rewarding, exciting and fun. Two types of motivation can be involved in learning. The first is outer or extrinsic motivation such as rewards, prizes, recognition, and approval. There is a place for some of this type of motivation in Sunday school teaching, but it should not be the only appeal used. It can imply that Biblical material is not important enough to be studied for its own worth.

A more acceptable approach to stimulate learning is to rely on inner or intrinsic motivation. The pupil's personal desires, drives, and interests are involved here. Learning is enhanced as the pupil is led to see how his needs are met through the application of Biblical principles in his life.

A LOOK AT TEACHING

If learning is a matter of change, of response, of inner, active, continuous, disciplined growth, of sensorial experience, of readiness and motivation, then what kind of teaching will result in this kind of learning? What is the role of the teacher?

Incomplete Concepts of Teaching

There are many different concepts that some teachers have of how to approach their students. Often the problem

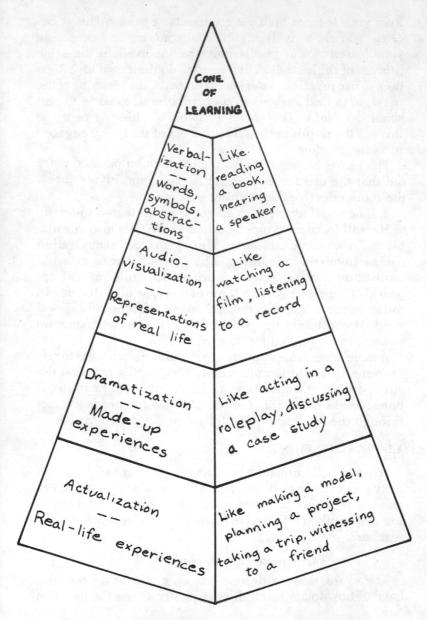

CONE OF LEARNING

Verbalization
--
Words, symbols, abstractions

Like reading a book, hearing a speaker

Audio-visualization
--
Representations of real life

Like watching a film, listening to a record

Dramatization
--
Made-up experiences

Like acting in a roleplay, discussing a case study

Actualization
--
Real-life experiences

Like making a model, planning a project, taking a trip, witnessing to a friend lies in focusing on one area to the exclusion of others. Let's look for some of these incomplete concepts of teaching.

Some teachers feel that with all their knowledge and experience, they have something important to say to their students. And so, they do all the talking in the classroom. They allow little opportunity for the students to raise questions or discuss problems of concern to them, or to discover spiritual truth on their own. They often have little contact with their students during the week.

An almost opposite approach is followed by the teacher who encourages the students to set the direction in the class. He may begin the session and then let the class take over when they come to something of interest to them. Such a teacher seldom has any kind of lesson aim or teaching plan.

Another teacher may depend on the curriculum material to guide his teaching. If it's in the quarterly, he'll do it; if it's not, forget it.

Still another teacher may feel like he has to drill things into his students if they are to learn. He uses various types of rote learning techniques in teaching the class.

Some teachers feel that since learning is an active process, their job is to keep the students busy doing something —anything, just so they're involved. Their class session is one continuous round of activity with little thought of the purpose of that activity or any clear teaching aims in mind.

And then there is the teacher who simply depends on the Holy Spirit to guide his session. Since he's involved in a spiritual ministry, he seldom spends much time in lesson preparation. He depends on the Holy Spirit to give him something to say when he stands before his class.

From these profiles we can learn some things that teaching is not. Teaching is not . . .

. . . Talking. Just because a teacher is talking and the pupils appear to be listening does not mean that real teaching and learning is taking place.

. . . Letting the students do all the talking either. Some students' comments are only a pooling of ignorance.

. . . Just covering the assigned lesson material. Just because a teacher has covered the assigned pages in his lesson quarterly for that Sunday does not mean he has fulfilled his role as a teacher.

. . . Cramming things into the pupils' heads without any thought of their impact on hearts and lives.

. . . Activity for activity's sake. Just because the students are actively involved does not mean they are learning anything of real value. There must be meaning and purpose to student activity.

. . . Relying on the Holy Spirit to make up for a lack of adequate preparation and planning. The Spirit can guide advance preparation as well as guide the activity of the moment.

. . . An exercise in spiritual superiority. A Christian teacher does not have to try to prove himself to be the source of all spiritual wisdom and understanding at the expense of the involvement of his students in the learning process.

. . . Not limited to 1 hour on Sunday morning. A teacher who can't wait for the bell to ring ending the class period, and who doesn't see or think about his students again until next Sunday, isn't much of a teacher. Some of the most effective teaching/learning situations often take place outside of the classroom.

Real Christian Teaching

Here is a group of words which, taken together, help to describe what real Christian teaching is:

Christian teaching is telling. Teaching is not *just* talking, but it is impossible to think of a teaching process that does not involve some use of the lecture method. True, many teachers have overemphasized this aspect, but it is still important to the Christian teacher. Part of the teacher's task is that of declaring and communicating divine truth. Therefore, he need never hesitate to give direct instruction where it is needed. A later chapter of this book will discuss some of the creative uses of the lecture method.

Christian teaching is guiding. If learning is an activity of self-discovery in which the pupil engages, then teaching is a matter of guiding the activities of the pupils so that desired learning takes place.

This approach to teaching may be compared with conducting a guided tour. The competent guide is familiar with all the points of interest, so he can help the group map out their itinerary and answer their questions. He facilitates the trip by making the necessary arrangements, and leads them to the main attractions so that every hour brings new experiences. The satisfaction of the tourists comes from their firsthand experiences with new people and places. (Lois E. LeBar, *op. cit.*, pp. 36, 37.)

The same is true of a good teacher. He knows the individual needs and interests of his pupils. He helps them discover Biblical truths for themselves and guides them to make personal applications. He supplies leading questions to bring out desired responses, but he never does anything for his pupils that they can more profitably do for themselves. He makes limited use of teacher-centered methods in favor of pupil-centered activities.

Christian teaching is sharing. The teacher, because he is usually more mature and advanced in spiritual matters, shares with the pupils his knowledge and experience. But he is not an all-knowing expert whose views cannot be challenged. Instead, he is an active, helping, thinking, searching member of the group.

This approach to teaching can even change the seating arrangement of the classroom. Instead of standing before his class, the teacher takes his place among the students, in a circular arrangement if possible.

Christian teaching is controlling. To say that teaching is a guiding, sharing process is not to say that it is uncontrolled or undisciplined. Learning is a disciplined process. It is the teacher's responsibility to maintain a reasonably controlled situation in which learning can take place. (Note: It says "a *reasonably* controlled situation," not a *rigidly* controlled situation.) The fact is that not all class discussion is profitable, not all pupils' comments are relative to the lesson study. The teacher must continually keep the class on the right track. And he must do so without offending the students.

Christian teaching is planning. Teaching is planning . . .
. . . purposeful lesson aims
. . . how to capture student interest
. . . stimulating learning activities
. . . how to actively involve the learner
. . . individual activities for different pupils
. . . the use of effective teaching methods
. . . how to use the learning environment creatively
. . . how to lead the pupils to desired responses.
This is the time for teacher activity—before the class. In the class it is the pupils who should be active, following through on the results of the teacher's planning and preparation.

Christian teaching is inspiring. One of the primary tasks of the teacher is that of motivating his pupils: motivating them to attend regularly, to study their lessons, to get involved in the learning process, to respond to that which they have learned.

Someone has defined the task of the teacher as that of "winning the attention of the unattentive, interesting the uninterested, and awakening the concern of the unconcerned." He must make learning interesting, challenging, satisfying, and fun.

Christian teaching is caring. A teacher will never be effective unless he genuinely loves and cares about his pupils. He will love them not as a group but as unique individuals facing personal problems, cherishing personal hopes and dreams. He will be interested not just in their spiritual needs but in every area of their lives. As far as is humanly possible, he will be fair in his dealings with his pupils. Some will be easy to love: the well-behaved, the well-groomed, those who share his point of view. Others will be harder to love: the undisciplined, the unkempt, the argumentative, the unlovely. These too he must love.

Someone has aptly paraphrased the last verse of 1 Corinthians 13 to read: "As a teacher I must possess knowledge, technique, and love, all three; but the greatest of these is love."

Christian teaching is living. Findley B. Edge has said, "The single most important factor that influences learning is the life and personality of the teacher." (Edge, *opt. cit.,* p. 223.) This is true because Christian truths are better understood when seen in life. Teaching techniques are of little use unless they are used by one through whose life the truth and love of God radiates. Everything about the teacher teaches: his attitudes, his actions, his ambitions, his affections, his appearance. This is what Paul meant when he wrote: "You are a letter from Christ . . . written not with ink but with the Spirit of the living God, not on tablets of stone but on tablets of human hearts" (2 Corinthians 3:3, RSV).

Students may not always study their lessons, but they do study the life of their teacher. That is why Christian teaching is really a matter of Christian living.

4 Teaching Methods to Use With Children

From what we have learned about the teaching/learning process up to this point, what can we assume about the use of teaching methods? First, we know that the most effective methods will be those that most closely relate to the way in which the pupils learn. If learning is an active process, then the methods must be participative methods, methods that involve the students.

Second, maybe we need to think of methods more as learning methods rather than as teaching methods. In other words, the teacher will use the methods that most enhance the learning of his students rather than those with which he is most comfortable or most skilled in using.

This section on methods divides the topic into three parts: teaching methods for children, teaching methods for youth and adults, and audiovisual methods.

USING STORYTELLING

One of the oldest teaching methods for children of all ages is the storytelling method. It has many values for the Christian teacher. Stories provide pleasure and enjoyment. They help change attitudes, stimulate emotions, and develop the imagination of the learner. Stories are an effective way to convey Biblical concepts to children. Students develop good habits of attention and learn to apply Biblical truths in their lives. They enlarge their experiences as they put themselves into the story situation. Stories help the students to see the results of good and bad choices made by the characters in the story.

Stories can be used to introduce a lesson, to illustrate a point, to apply the lesson to life, to lead to worship, to introduce a song, to teach Scripture memorization, and so on.

Parts and Structure of a Story

A story can be divided into four basic parts:

Introduction. The introduction seeks to arouse interest and attention. Characters and settings are presented and the problem or conflict is introduced. This part of the story should be brief and not too complicated. The teacher should plan for variety in introducing the story, something other than, "Once upon a time." Occasionally try a startling statement or direct conversation such as, " 'What am I doing here?' thought Joseph as he paced across his cell."

Body. This is where the main events of the story unfold. Be sure to get things in their proper sequence. Nothing kills a good story as quickly as, "Oh yes, I forgot to tell you—while they were in the cave. . . . " Be careful to avoid side issues. Keep the details simple, especially for young children. The body of the story should build in suspense.

Climax. Here is where the solution to the problem or the secret to the plot is revealed. This is where suspense and interest must climax.

Conclusion. As the story ends, characters must be disposed of and minds put at ease. And it should end as quickly as it began—without moralizing. A good story should not have to be explained. The emphasis or impact should be so obvious that everyone gets the point.

Selecting stories. The stories you tell should be worth telling. They must have a spiritual purpose and be true to the Bible. The students must be able to identify with the characters and events of the story, which means that the story must be appropriate to the age-group.

Preschoolers enjoy stories about familiar things from their daily experiences. They like stories about babies, pets, children their own age, family groups. Choose Bible stories carefully for this age-group. Limit the story to one thought or idea. Stories should not be longer than the group attention span of the young child—2 to 5 minutes for nursery children and 5 to 10 minutes for beginners.

Primaries like fantasy stories about animals that talk or trees that move, while juniors want their stories to be realistic and true to life. Nearly all the Bible stories are appropriate for these ages. The attention span for primaries is up to 15 minutes and up to 20 minutes for juniors.

Preparing to Tell a Story

Learn and relearn the story. Read the story from several versions of the Bible and from children's Bible storybooks. Study the plot and the sequence of events. Try to envision the setting and the characters of the story. Cut or elaborate on the story according to your needs and purpose.

Think through the story in its four parts. Write out the introduction and conclusion and outline the main events of the story.

Practice telling the story aloud. Tell it over and over until your presentation becomes natural. Use a mirror to improve your style.

Principles of Storytelling

Storytelling is an art, but an art that, with a little effort, every teacher can learn to develop.

1. Assume a natural position at eye level with the pupils. Maintain eye contact.

2. Use a few natural gestures. Avoid distracting mannerisms.

3. Be enthusiastic. Make the story come alive.

4. Use direct discourse by changing the tone of your voice to represent the different characters. This makes it unnecessary to say repeatedly, "And David said . . ." "And the giant said . . ."

5. Use language the student can easily understand. Use

simple, action words. Don't talk down to the students.
6. Enunciate clearly and articulately. Project your voice so all can hear.
7. Change the pace and volume of your delivery. Use an occasional pause to heighten suspense and refocus attention.
8. Tell the story. Don't read it.

Variety in Storytelling

Instead of always using the flannelboard, try a shallow pan of sand to set the figures in. Or use a lapboard—a piece of styrofoam with slits cut into it to hold the figures. It may be necessary to back the figures with a strip of cardboard to make them stand upright.

For variety use a prerecorded story tape or record to tell the story. Also use filmstrips and storystrips on the "show-'n'-tell" viewer.

Use a hand-puppet character to tell the story, use puppets to depict the characters of the story, or draw stick figures on the chalkboard.

Use a story rug or backdrop to create a story area in the room or department. When you move to this area, the children learn to settle down and get ready to listen.

Involving the Children in the Story

Storytelling is primarily a matter of teacher activity, so how can we involve the pupil in the learning process? Let the children act out the story. Little or no costuming is necessary. Repeat the action with different pupils playing the lead roles. With preschoolers several children can play one part at the same time. Young children also enjoy finger play or acting out the story.

The entire class could be involved in acting out the story. For example, in the story of Noah several students could act out the parts of Noah and his sons; some of the children could pretend to be the pairs of animals entering the ark; others could play the part of the mocking crowd; while the rest of the group makes the sounds of wind and rain (by finger drumming on a tabletop). The words of God should be read directly from the Bible.

Or let the children tell the story and put the figures on the flannelboard or manipulate the puppets.

Encourage the children to draw some scene from the story or mold the characters from clay. Or they could select several pictures to illustrate the story. Have them make up a song about the story. This works well with primary children. Older children can write their own life-situation story based on a Bible story.

USING LEARNING CENTERS

An effective approach to teaching children is the use of learning centers. Learning centers actually involve the use of a wide variety of teaching methods.

Learning Centers–What Are They?

Interest centers, station learning, individualized instruction, Bible-learning activities, open classrooms—all of these terms are used to define the learning center approach.

Basically, a learning center is a place where students become involved in direct learning activities which reinforce the Bible lesson. A learning center may be as sophisticated as a listening carrel with tape recorders and multiple headphone sets, or as simple as a table with paper and crayons, or a bird's nest in the nature corner.

Learning Centers—Why Use Them?

Discovery learning. We have already seen that the rate of learning increases proportionately to the learner's level of involvement, and learning centers provide a high level of involvement. Students would rather find the answer than be told or shown it. They want to be eager participants, not just casual observers.

Choice. In the learning center approach children are given the opportunity and responsibility to make choices. They may choose one learning center over another or one type of activity or resource over another. This doesn't mean they can do as they please. Instead, they are learning to make choices within certain limits.

Development. Learning centers encourage the students to develop their skills, interests, and abilities. Often these skills are usable outside the classroom in independent Bible study and sharing.

Variety. Learning centers provide for a maximum of variety. Each week brings new activities and projects. The lesson truth is approached from different reference points using a variety of media and resources.

Senses. Learning centers provide for a wide range of sensorial experiences—touch, sight, hearing, smell, even taste. The involvement of the senses is especially important in teaching preschoolers.

Sharing. Students are given an opportunity to share the results of their group or individual work. Learning center projects are often used in department worship, service projects, at home, and so on. Children also learn to share and help each other as they work in small groups.

Attitudes. The use of learning centers helps develop positive attitudes toward Sunday school, church, and spiritual things. Students learn that studying the Bible in the relaxed, interesting atmosphere of the learning center is a pleasant and rewarding experience. Discipline problems are usually minimal. The children are too busy having a good time to get into trouble.

Individualized. Students are able to work at their own pace according to their individual interests and abilities. Teachers have time to give personal help and attention to the pupils.

Creativity. The students are encouraged to think for themselves and to engage in creative learning experiences. Teachers, too, are challenged to use innovative approaches to communicate ideas and Biblical principles.

Teachers. The learning center approach allows the teacher

to fulfill his role as a guide of the learning process. Learning centers promote the team teaching concept as workers plan the learning activities for their department or class together. It also allows the teachers to work in their area of specialization. This approach provides an excellent means of teacher training as new workers are used to assist group activities. The pupils have opportunity to relate to several teachers instead of just one.

Learning Centers—How to Use Them

The best way to understand the operation of the learning center approach may be to move step-by-step through the planning and presentation phases.

Quarterly and unit planning. Planning is first done on a whole quarter basis. The department superintendent or team leader distributes the new curriculum materials to his teachers and sets a time and place for a planning meeting. All the workers are expected to become familiar with the lessons for the quarter beforehand. At the meeting the workers decide on the aim and emphasis for the quarter. They also note how the lessons of the quarter are divided into units of two or more lessons. They then proceed with planning the first unit of study, repeating some of the same procedures as above in determining emphasis, objectives, and so on.

Lesson planning. The teaching team also meets on a monthly or weekly basis to plan the individual lessons. The first step again is to select a lesson aim. This aim becomes the theme for the learning centers that will be used in that session. Next they decide how the basic Bible story or Scripture passage will be presented. This may involve storytelling, listening to the story on tape or record, viewing a filmstrip, working in small Bible study groups, etc.

The next step is to plan a series of activities and interest centers that will reenforce the Bible lessons and give opportunity for the students to make discoveries for themselves. These may include drama or art centers, resource centers, music and worship, visuals, etc. Both the teacher's curriculum materials and the age-levels section of the *SS Action* magazine can be used as resources for ideas.

The team of workers must make specific assignments and begin preparing the different learning centers. They must secure the necessary materials and supplies such as pictures, records, filmstrips, art supplies, objects, and so on. And they must make sure the learning centers are set up prior to the Sunday school session. The centers should be made to look attractive and inviting.

Presentation. The class session may begin with individualized, small group, or large group activities. The students may go directly to one of the interest centers, or the entire class or department may meet to find out what the theme is for the lesson and what learning centers are available for that day. The pattern will often vary.

Instructions may be shared with the whole group, or written or verbal directions may be shared with the students as they arrive at the learning center.

Each center will be staffed by at least one worker who will assist and guide the students as needed, discuss the lesson or other matters of interest with them, and observe their work at the center.

The session may close with the students still in the learning centers, or the group can meet in a closing assembly for worship and to share the results of their learning center work.

Evaluation. The final step is evaluation. The staff meets to consider some of the following questions: 1) Were the learning center activities suitable to the age-level and abilities of our students? 2) Did they fit our aim for this lesson? 3) Did they stimulate interest and motivate learning? 4) Were the activities worth the investment in time and effort? 5) Did we adequately plan and pray to ensure the success of the activities? 6) What insights have we gained about our students?

Other Questions About Learning Centers

What facilities do we need? A large open area is most ideal. Learning centers can be set up throughout the room as shown in diagram #1.

A large assembly area surrounded by smaller classrooms can be easily used by setting up learning centers in the room and assembly area. (See diagram #2.)

A group of small classrooms off a central hall can also be used with learning centers. Individual rooms can be set up with different activities, the wall space in the hall used for display areas. A unified decorating theme can be used to tie the area together.

Existing facilities can be adapted to accommodate learning centers by removing some nonbearing walls to make larger areas. Support posts can be used to replace bearing walls. The doors can be removed from small rooms to facilitate freer movement through the interest centers. All unnecessary equipment such as large tables and bulky storage cabinets should be removed to provide more open floorspace. These can be replaced with smaller folding tables or with tables hinged to the walls which can be dropped down when not in use.

Some of the basic equipment needed for learning centers are tables and chairs, shelving, art easels, bulletin boards, and housekeeping and block centers in the preschool departments.

What other resources do we need? These will include books, maps, pictures, magazines, records, tapes, sheet and roll paper, art supplies, modeling clay, crayons, felt pens, scissors, etc.

Audiovisual equipment such as tape recorders and headphones, filmstrip and "show 'n' tell" viewers, overhead and slide projectors are valuable resources, but they are not absolutely essential in beginning the learning center approach.

The fact is most Sunday schools could begin using learn-

PRESCHOOL CLASSROOM ARRANGEMENTS USING INTEREST CENTERS
Accommodations for 30 children: approximately 900-1,000 sq. ft.

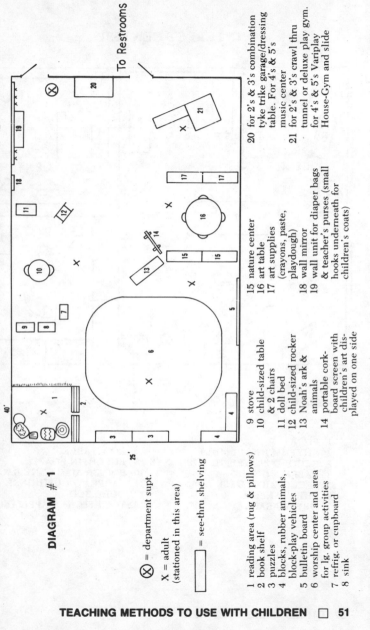

DIAGRAM # 1

To Restrooms

⊗ = department supt.

X = adult
(stationed in this area)

▭ = see-thru shelving

1 reading area (rug & pillows)
2 book shelf
3 puzzles
4 blocks, rubber animals,
  block-play vehicles
5 bulletin board
6 worship center and area
  for lg. group activities
7 refrig. or cupboard
8 sink

9 stove
10 child-sized table
   & 2 chairs
11 doll bed
12 child-sized rocker
13 Noah's ark &
   animals
14 portable cork-
   board screen with
   children's art dis-
   played on one side

15 nature center
16 art table
17 art supplies
   (crayons, paste,
   playdough)
18 wall mirror
19 wall unit for diaper bags
   & teacher's purses (small
   hooks underneath for
   children's coats)

20 for 2's & 3's combination
   tyke trike garage/dressing
   table. For 4's & 5's
   music center
21 for 2's & 3's crawl thru
   tunnel or deluxe play gym.
   for 4's & 5's Variplay
   House-Gym and slide

INTEREST CENTERS

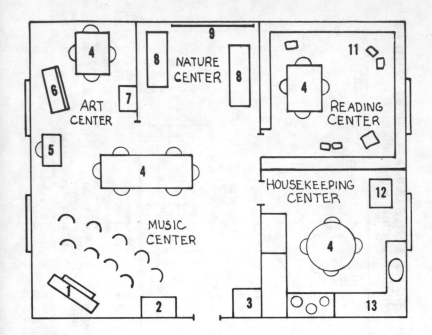

DIAGRAM # 2

1. PIANO
2. RHYTHM INSTRUMENT
3. RECORD PLAYER, HEADPHONES
4. TABLE & CHAIRS
5. SECRETARY'S DESK
6. ART EASELS
7. DRYING RACK
8. LOW TABLE
9. BULLETIN BOARD
10. BOOK & MAGAZINE RACKS
11. CARPET & CUSHIONS
12. DOLL BED
13. TOY KITCHEN APPLIANCES

ing centers with the facilities and resources they already have. Innovation is the key, not expensive equipment.

What curriculum can we use? The Word of Life (Gospel Publishing House) curriculum is readily adaptable to the learning center approach. The elementary materials have been revised with this approach in mind. Many of the teaching activities suggested in the curriculum can be used in learning centers.

How do we schedule for learning centers? The learning center approach works best with a 2-hour combined Sunday school and children's church (extended session) time period. But it can also be used with only a 1-hour session if most of the time is given to teaching activities.

There are several scheduling options available: 1) Use learning centers throughout the entire session. During this time the students work with the activities of their choice. This works well with younger preschool children. 2) Students can rotate from one center to another according to a predetermined schedule. 3) Use whole department activities for part of the session and learning centers for part of the session. The class or department may meet together for music, storytelling, and worship and move to learning centers for memory work, handwork, research, playtime, etc.

How would we begin a learning center approach in our Sunday school? It is usually best to begin with a pilot program in one department. Facilities and equipment need to be provided for and arranged beforehand. Workers need to be trained. This may be provided by suggesting books and articles to read, visiting a church or school in the area that is using learning centers, or working with a teacher who is experienced in using learning centers. Parents and pupils need to be oriented to the learning center approach. This can be done through letters, open house, lab sessions, etc.

What are some of the basic learning centers? The following is a brief description of some of the various learning centers that could be provided. Obviously not all of these activities would be offered at the same time or with the same age-groups. These learning centers will often be used in combination with each other. Plan on one learning center for each group of 5-8 children.

Story center. Here is where the Bible story for the session is told. It may include a story rug, flannelboard supplies, hand puppets, filmstrip projector, etc.

Listening center. Here students listen to Bible stories or music on tape or record. This area may include record and tape players, headphone sets, tabletop viewer sets, "show-'n'-tell" viewer.

Book center. Children come to this area to look at picture books or read Bible or life-application stories. A worker is needed here to read stories to nonreaders.

Research center. This area would contain Bible study helps such as a concordance, dictionary, atlas, etc. Students come here to look up information related to the lesson.

Arts and crafts center. Activities and supplies in this center would include easel painting, finger painting, crayon or chalk drawing, poster making, clay modeling, unit projects, and so on.

Housekeeping center. This learning center would only be provided for the preschool departments. It would include small kitchen appliances, such as a play stove, refrigerator, tables, dishes, dolls, etc. Old clothes may be provided for dress-up play. The housekeeping center helps the young child relate Christian concepts to everyday living.

Building center. This center, which would only be provided in the preschool departments, would include building blocks and other construction toys. The children may build a house or temple referred to in the lesson. Or they may build the "walls of Jericho" and march around them like the Israelites. The building center, besides helping the children relate to specific elements of the story, provides ways for them to learn to play together and be responsible for putting things away.

Nature center. This area may include small plants, animals in cages or aquariums, display items like birds' nests, bark, leaves, insect specimens, food samples, science pictures, etc. The children could also plant seeds and watch them grow. Here is where they can learn about the wonders of God's creation.

Music center. Activities in this area may include playing in a rhythm band, listening to music records or tapes, learning about hymns, selecting songs for a worship service, writing a new song, singing songs and action choruses. It may include songbooks, hymn storybooks, piano, autoharp or guitar, rhythm instruments, and so on.

Snack center. Preschool children appreciate a snack sometime during the morning. This too can be a learning experience as they thank God for their food. Foods may be selected that relate to the lesson such as bread with the feeding of the multitude or pieces of fruit with the lessons on Creation. Supplies and equipment needed include disposable plates and cups, paper towels, bibs for the youngest children, a variety of crackers, small cookies, juice, etc.

Drama center. At the drama center students can act out or pantomime stories, roleplay different situations, plan a skit, etc. Some simple costuming may also be kept in the drama center like bathrobes, turbans, or different kinds of hats.

Viewing center. Various kinds of equipment could be used here such as "show-'n'-tell" projectors, view master or tabletop filmstrip viewers. Supplies could be kept here for students to make their own write-on slides or filmstrips or overhead transparencies. Inexpensive viewing carrels can be made from large cardboard boxes.

Writing center. Activities here give the students opportunity to express the lesson in their own words. Older primaries and juniors may write poems, newspaper stories, letters, scripts for a play or slide series. Equipment would include tables and chairs or lapboards, pencils, paper, etc.

Missions center. At this center the students can study about the life and work of missionaries and the different countries in which they work. Supplies would include maps, curios, a bulletin board for letters to and from missionaries,

BGMC posters, missions costumes, etc. This is where the BGMC bank may be set up to collect the children's offerings each month. Visiting missionaries and their families could meet at this area to talk with the students.

Memory center. Students come to this area to work on Bible memory assignments related to the lessons. Supplies may include quiz games, flash cards, scrambled word puzzles, a chart of memory work progress, tape recorders to use in reciting verses. The students may work at setting verses to music or working up a choral reading of the verses they know.

Can we use learning centers with youth and adults? The learning center approach is used most often in the children's departments, but it has definite application in teaching older students. Learning centers with youth and adults may take the form of projects and work groups. The entire hour would not be used for learning centers. The students may begin the session in work groups and reassemble later, or begin in a large group for the Bible lesson presentation and then divide into small groups to do further research or plan applicational activities. With more skills and resources, youth and adults could develop some very sophisticated projects such as making slide presentations with full narration, writing and presenting a play, planning a class field trip, etc.

USING BIBLE-LEARNING GAMES

Many games can be used as aids to teaching and learning. Popular TV games such as "Password" or "What's My Line?" can be adapted to the Sunday school using Bible words and characters.

Quiz games can be used to test factual knowledge. These can be made more interesting by using the "Bible Baseball" approach where players advance around the bases and score points with each correct answer; or by using various kinds of gaming techniques such as crossword puzzles, riddles, codes, etc. The students' creative abilities can be tapped in enlisting their help in thinking up many of these games and puzzles.

Memory work can be aided by using scrambled word games in which the students correctly arrange the words, or matching games in which the verse on one piece of paper or wooden stick must be matched with the correct reference. Flash cards can also be used to make memory work fun.

5 Teaching Methods to Use With Youth and Adults

A young child from a Christian home often has little or no choice as to whether he is going to attend Sunday school or not. But the same is not true of older youth and adults. What parental pressure may have been exerted on a youth living at home is no longer a factor once he leaves home. Young adults are breaking many old habits, one of which may be that of attending Sunday school. This means they must be motivated to attend for other reasons. They must want to come because they find satisfying personal relationships there, because they find their needs met, because the study lessons are interesting, because they are involved in the learning process.

"But aren't youth and adults old enough to just sit still and listen?" Yes, they may be old enough to "sit still," but while they are "sitting and listening," their minds may be miles away. They may not create a discipline problem as a young child might, but they may be totally unaware of, and uninvolved with, what is going on in the classroom. Involvement learning is as important with youth and adults as it is with children.

Of course, many of the methods used with youth and adults will be quite different from those used with children. Actually the methods used with older students have more potential for involvement. This is because older students have more resources and experiences to bring to the teaching/learning situation.

In this chapter we will briefly discuss some of the basic

methods in four major categories and then explore some of the more creative, participative adaptions of these basic techniques.

CREATIVE USE OF LECTURE METHODS

No method is more widely used, and at the same time more widely criticized, than the lecture method. It is one of the most difficult methods to use effectively. Yet it remains one of the teacher's basic tools of the trade.

There are a number of advantages to using the lecture method. It is a good way to cover a large amount of material in a short amount of time. It provides for logical, systematic coverage of a subject. It is also useful in teaching a large class. The teacher retains control of the teaching/learning situation. He can also project the power of his personality into the lecture.

Of course, there are also some limitations in using the lecture method. It permits a minimum of pupil participation and response. The teacher has little or no feedback from the students. Extensive use of the lecture method tends to stifle student initiative and creativity.

The problems inherent in the use of lecture may not always lie with the method itself but with its use by the teacher. Here are some principles that may result in more effective use of the lecture: 1) The method works best in combination with other methods such as to introduce a role-play situation, to give an assignment, or to summarize a discussion. 2) The lecturer will be more effective if he speaks from a clear simple outline, uses interesting illustrations, and tries to anticipate and include the questions his students may raise. 3) The lecture should be supported with visual aids to help retain attention and emphasize the main points. Some teachers prefer to prepare and distribute a mimeographed outline of their lecture. 4) Practice of good principles of speaking such as eye contact and voice inflection will increase the effectiveness of the lecture method. It is important, too, that students maintain good posture during a lecture. (Kenneth Gangel, *24 Ways to Improve Youth Teaching* [Wheaton: Victor Books, 1974], p. 15.)

Adaptations of the Lecture Methods

Listening teams. Involvement in the lecture method can be sparked by dividing the class into teams to each listen to the lecture with a different question in mind. This technique gives the students something specific to listen for. Listening teams can also be used when viewing a film or filmstrip or listening to a record or tape recording. The teacher must structure a set of questions and make the team assignments before the lecture or audiovisual presentation.

Colloquy. This technique is used following the lecture. The class is divided into small groups to discuss what they have just heard and compile a list of questions. Then a representative from each group becomes part of a panel to address the questions to the lecturer.

Research and report. In every class there are some students who have special areas of ability or access to resources that would be of interest to the rest of the class. These persons may not be qualified to serve as a regular teacher, but they can be tapped, using the research and report method. This technique encourages home study and benefits the class by bringing in outside findings and introducing a new personality into the teaching team. The assignment must be made far enough in advance so the student will have time to do his research and prepare his report. The teacher should offer help as to sources, outlines, and so on.

Symposium. The symposium is an extension of the research and report method involving two or more persons who each speak in turn on one aspect of an assigned topic. The symposium works best on those topics which have several easy subdivisions. For example, when surveying an entire book of the Bible, several students could be assigned to each speak on one part of the book outline. The symposium speakers should know exactly how much time they have to make their presentation.

Guest speaker. Another way to achieve variety in the lecture method is to use an occasional guest speaker. Visiting ministers, evangelists, missionaries, or specialists in a field such as history, government, etc., can be invited to speak to the class. The teacher may let the guest speaker choose his topic or direct him to a particular subject. Time should be allowed for questions from the class.

Dialogue-interview. In the dialogue method two people discuss a topic before the rest of the group. The participants may be a team of teachers, a teacher and a pupil, or two pupils. If the teacher wishes to retain control of the teaching situation, he may choose to interview the guest speaker himself. In this way he can direct the conversation to areas he feels would be of interest and benefit to his class. The students may also ask questions. The purpose of the dialogue-interview is to discuss the feelings, understanding, options, or reactions of another person.

Debate. A debate is a somewhat more formal presentation in which two persons or teams each speak in turn from opposing viewpoints. The debate can then be followed by an open discussion of the subject by the rest of the class.

Storytelling. This method has definite applications for teaching youth and adults. Some variations are:

Open-ended stories in which the class can suggest various endings using principles from the lesson.

Case studies are true or hypothetical situations common to the everyday lives of the students. This method gives the students experience in applying Biblical lesson truths to real-life situations.

Current events can be used to introduce a lesson or to illustrate a point. The students could be assigned to look for newsstories to clip and bring to class.

Personal experiences or things that have happened in the lives of the teacher or pupils. These should be used somewhat sparingly.

Illustrations and stories from church history, missions, world or American history, or literature can be used.

Bible story filmstrips can also occasionally be used with youth and adults.

CREATIVE USE OF DISCUSSION METHODS

The discussion method is one of the most popular methods of teaching. People like to talk, and discussion gives them opportunity to do so in a productive manner. The discussion method also offers many possibilities for participation in the learning process. It involves both group and individual activity. It helps students learn to crystallize their thinking and express themselves verbally. It helps them to feel at ease with, and part of, the group; and it can cause them to change their thinking and behavior to align with the group. It also provides a means of feedback to the teacher.

There are some limitations in the use of the discussion method. As Ken Gangel says, it can become a *"substitute* rather than a *supplement* to the proclamation of the Word of God."* (Gangel, *op. cit.*, p. 34.) In-depth discussion can be time-consuming. Sometimes the discussion can wander and become merely aimless talk. Conclusions can be incomplete or even incorrect. Some students may be reluctant to join the discussion. Some seating arrangements make it difficult to use the discussion method.

Many of these problems can be solved if the teacher will follow some basic principles for leading effective discussions.

1. He must plan the discussion to center on a problem or situation the students can identify with and become personally involved in.

2. There must be a purpose for the discussion. The leader must know where he wants to go with the discussion.

3. He must construct good, thought-provoking questions.

4. He must plan a good introduction to the discussion, possibly using a technique like an open-ended story, a case study, or roleplaying.

5. The discussion leader should maintain a relaxed, ac-

cepting atmosphere in which the students feel free to respond, and encourage each one to participate.

6. He must keep the discussion moving and on the subject at hand.

7. He must keep a few students from monopolizing the discussion. It may be necessary to remind the participants of this fact beforehand. Occasionally, he may call on specific individuals to respond. Or he may say, "Let's hear from someone who hasn't said anything yet."

8. The leader should summarize the main points of the discussion and restate the conclusion of the group.

A common problem in posing questions for discussion is to make them too simple, too general, too difficult, or too personal. Good questions require careful thought. They must be brief, clear, and specific.

Too often if the teacher does not get an immediate answer to a question, he either restates it or answers it himself. If a question requires real thought, the teacher should be willing to give his students time to think.

Another common problem in using questions is: What do you do when you get the wrong response? A wise teacher will use what may be right in the reply and then call on others for further information. Or he may take the blame for wording the question poorly and restate it. In this way he does not make the pupil feel bad for giving an incorrect answer.

Adaptations of the Discussion Method

Panel—A panel is an informal discussion carried on by representatives of the group with the participants seated in front of the class. The value of this technique is that several viewpoints can be presented. In selecting persons to serve on a panel the teacher may deliberately choose those with varying shades of opinion.

Several different types of panels are:

The *guided panel* in which the moderator directs the questions to the panel members and keeps the discussion on track.

The *self-guided panel* in which the members discuss a topic they have studied beforehand without a moderator.

The *impromptu panel* in which the members are selected from the group with no prior notice or preparation. The purpose of this technique is to secure opinions and reactions.

The *expanding panel* in which the members rotate into the panel from the audience. The purpose is to seek other viewpoints on the topic.

Buzz groups are small discussion groups of from three to eight persons each discussing simultaneously various phases of a topic with group reports to follow. It is a good way to discover solutions to a given problem. It also achieves wide pupil participation and helps to overcome the timidity of some who would be hesitant to respond in a large group.

The teacher should: appoint a leader and a recorder for each group; supply each group with specific instructions or questions to guide their discussion; check on each group to see that they are on the subject and making progress; and set a definite time limit for the buzz groups.

Some seating arrangements do not readily lend themselves to this method. Where there is fixed seating such as in an auditorium, buzz groups can be set up in the aisles, at the end of two or three rows of seats, or at the back or front of the room.

Dyads or "couple buzzers" are a variation of the buzz group involving just two persons. The class is divided into dyads for a brief period of time (1-2 minutes) to discuss an assigned topic or suggest solutions to a problem. The teacher may or may not call for reports from each group. Dyads work well in a large group where it is impractical to use buzz groups or where small-group seating cannot be arranged.

Circle response. This method calls for a response from each class member in turn, going around the room or table. No one is permitted to respond twice until all have spoken once. This technique gives each class member opportunity to participate and to hear what everyone else in the group is thinking. If some would rather not respond it is, of course, best not to insist that they do so.

Brainstorming. The purpose of brainstorming is to generate numerous responses to a question or problem and to create an accepting attitude that may encourage further participation. All responses to a question are listed on the chalkboard without immediate evaluation. Then the teacher and class go back over the list and remove those that may not be appropriate. In this way the student who offered an answer that was rejected is not so closely associated with this response because of the time lapse between writing it down and evaluating it.

Agree-disagree. In this method students indicate their agreement or disagreement with a set of statements or questions that may have valid pro or con issues. The statements are purposely worded somewhat vaguely to provoke discussion. Students may indicate their opinions by raising their hands, standing to their feet, or moving to the "agree" or "disagree" side of the room. This method works well to introduce a topic and to generate lively discussion.

Direct group Bible study. This method can be used often with older children, youth, and adults. The students work in small groups to discuss a Bible passage using questions supplied by the teacher such as: To whom was the passage addressed? What did it mean to them? What problems or needs existed? What does the passage say to us? What response does it call for? What action should we take?

CREATIVE USE OF DRAMA

Drama is an excellent creative learning activity. Bible stories and situations come alive. Students become involved, mentally, physically, and emotionally. Drama helps develop creativity and stimulate thought, discussion, and response. Youth and adults gain insights into the character and actions of others.

Hurst and Turner suggest six basic steps in using drama as

a teaching method: 1) Information—Students must know the story or understand the situation; 2) Discussion—Must precede and follow the presentation; 3) Decision—Students must be involved in deciding how to make the presentation; 4) Planning—A must for effective learning through drama; 5) Production—The group must not become so preoccupied with the process that they lose sight of its purpose—that of reinforcing learning; 6) Evaluation—Questions to ask are: What was done? Why and how? With what results? (Hurst and Turner, *op. cit.*, p. 56.)

Adaptation of Drama

Skits are short presentations, usually with at least a partial script or brief rehearsal.

Plays are a more elaborate presentation, including several scenes or acts, costuming, scenery, rehearsals, and so on.

Pantomimes are actions which convey a message without dialogue or narration.

Pageants are reenactments of events accompanied by a narration. Costuming and staging may be used.

Tableaus are living pictures. Players assume a pose and hold it without action or words.

Demonstrations offer firsthand experience in "how to do it." Witnessing to a friend or using a concordance might be the topic of a demonstration.

Period interviews involve students in playing the roles of historical or Biblical characters. Other students then ask them questions about events of their day. For example several "reporters" from Jerusalem could interview Saul of Tarsus following the stoning of Stephen. The value of this method is that it makes Biblical and historical scenes come alive and also taps the imaginative and creative abilities of the students.

Roleplaying is an extemporaneous portrayal of a problem. The value of this method is that it allows the group to see and feel a real problem situation so they can discuss it more objectively. It also permits students to express emotions and feelings in a "make-believe" situation that they may not otherwise be willing to express. The steps involved in role-playing are: 1) Define the situation; 2) Assign the roles; 3) Brief the players and the group; 4) Enact the situation; 5) Cut off the action; 6) Discuss the scene. The players should be instructed as to what attitudes they are to display but should be left to act out the situation spontaneously. Following a discussion of the problem, the participants may replay the scene using the solutions suggested by the group.

CREATIVE USE OF PROJECT METHODS

Projects can be one of the most effective teaching methods because they involve the students in direct learning activities. They make learning fun, interesting, and more lasting and provide an outlet for expression and service. Projects also help to develop leadership abilities and promote fellowship among the learners. Projects may be done inside or outside of the classroom; they may involve individuals, small work groups, or the entire class or department; and they may last for only one class period or the whole quarter.

Some principles to keep in mind in using projects are:

1. Be sure to plan far enough in advance and make adequate preparation.

2. Involve the students in proposing, planning, and carrying out projects. They will take greater responsibility if they feel it is *their* project and not the *teacher's*.

3. The teacher serves as a resource person offering advice, information, and encouragement.

4. Don't start a project unless you intend to complete it. Let the students know you expect them to finish their projects.

Adaptations of the Project Method

There are basically three kinds of projects.

Projects that inform such as written answers to study questions, compiling a list of references from a concordance, field studies, etc.

Projects that change habits such as a program of regular personal Bible reading, a personal evaluation of some area of spiritual need, etc.

Projects that provide service such as making gifts for shut-ins, working around the church, conducting a service at a rest home, etc.

Field trips can be an effective learning experience, providing firsthand observation of a situation. Some things to do in planning a field trip are: 1) Discuss the trip before going; 2) Decide on the purpose of the trip and what to look for; 3) Make the necessary arrangements at the place of destination, with the parents, for transportation, etc.; 4) Discuss the trip after you return.

Writing projects. There are numerous writing projects to use with youth and adults such as:

Character comparison—Students compare or contrast two Biblical characters such as David and Saul.

Log or diary—Students compile a diary as it might have been kept by a Biblical character, such as Daniel.

Newspaper story—Students write a news account as it might have appeared in a local newspaper, such as an account of Jonah preaching in Ninevah, or design an ad as it might have appeared in a newspaper or magazine.

Parable—Students write a contemporary story which parallels a Biblical event or expresses how a Biblical principle can be applied in life.

Prayers—Students compose a written prayer expressing a need, thanksgiving, praise, etc. These could be used in a closing worship service.

Letters—Students write a letter to themselves explaining a change they need to make in their lives. The letters are put in envelopes addressed to themselves. The teacher sends the letters to the students during the week or at the end of the quarter.

Sensory response. Students read a Bible story and write down a color, a sound, and a smell that the event causes them to think of. Each person then explains why he wrote what he did.

Paraphrase. Students write a personal paraphrase of a brief Bible passage putting the thoughts of the verse into their own words. Or they can paraphrase the words of a familiar hymn.

Songwriting. Students write lyrics to a familiar melody or set a Bible verse to music.

Song titles. Compile a list of song titles which illustrate contemporary thinking on a subject such as "love." These can be contrasted with a list of sacred or gospel song titles on the same topic.

CHOOSING METHODS

Several questions a teacher should ask himself as he selects the methods he will use are:

1. Will it help me accomplish my aim for this session?
2. Is it appropriate to the age and experience of my students?
3. Will it work in our classroom or department?
4. Is the special equipment and materials I might need available?
5. Do I have enough time to use this method?

Remember, there is no one "best" or "worst" method. The worst methods are the ones used all the time. The best methods are those used with variety and in combination with others.

6 Using Audiovisual Aids

"And There Were Ten Teachers"

The average Sunday school is likened unto 10 teachers who took their lesson materials on a Sunday morning and went forth to meet their pupils. And five of them were wise and five were foolish.

They that were foolish took only their quarterlies and took no teaching aids with them. But the wise took many types of teaching aids and supplies along with their quarterlies and their Bibles.

And the wise teachers preceded their pupils to the classroom. And verily the boys and girls were quiet as they entered the room. Each pupil began to work at interesting projects and activities.

One wise teacher had a table with magazine pictures of animals who hide. And behold the boys and girls knew much information that they could share too. Soon the wise teacher told of Achan hiding his sin.

Verily, another wise teacher brought a newspaper headline that mentioned the Middle East and the pupils looked at maps until they found where Achan abode.

And likewise the third wise teacher made a white sugar lump turn black. And many boys and girls said unto her, "Sin is awful."

And at the art center the fourth wise teacher directed the pupils to take crayons and draw exceeding great things with circles and lines. And they knew that it was Jericho and the tents and Achan hiding his sin.

At the story center the fifth wise teacher showed flannel-graph figures of important little things—David's stones, the widow's two mites, the boy's basket, and the important little thing in Achan's life.

Behold, the teaching aids were many for one story. And these children said, "Learning about God is fun. We will come back and bring others with us."

And when the classes were over, the five foolish teachers arose and said unto the wise, "Give us of your ideas, for our attendance has gone down."

And the wise answered saying, "It is so. Teaching aids are good to have. Let us sit down one with another this week and talk about some of the different things that can be done."

WHY AUDIOVISUAL AIDS

We live in an audiovisual world. We are constantly bombarded with sights and sounds—television, billboards, public address systems, flashing lights. At times it can become mind boggling, but it is one of the ways in which we learn. So audiovisuals must be included in our study of effective teaching and learning.

In chapter 3 we said that learning is a "sensorial" experience in that the pupil learns through his senses. We discovered that a pupil remembers only 10 percent of what he hears and up to 90 percent of what he sees, hears, says, and does. These statistics, too, have something to say about the importance of using a variety of teaching and learning aids, those which involve a combination of the senses.

Teaching aids serve several important purposes. They (1) help arouse student interest and hold attention; (2) clarify words and ideas; (3) stimulate thought, imagination, and discussion; (4) provide a common experience for the whole group; (5) make learning more permanent; (6) provide for review and repetition.

Teaching aids are not an end in themselves but are a means to an end. They are not a time filler or a side issue but are designed to reinforce learning. They should not dominate the presentation but are a supplement to the lesson.

TEACHING AIDS OR LEARNING AIDS?

We most often think of audiovisuals as an aid to the teacher. But if we refocus our attention from the teacher to the pupil, then maybe we should refer to them as learning aids rather than as teaching aids. This concept may help us to think more about the pupil as we prepare our lessons and supporting audiovisual aids.

NONPROJECTED VISUAL AIDS

There are numerous, inexpensive nonprojected visual aids that are available to every teacher.

Chalkboard

Every good teacher should make wide use of the chalkboard. He should leave his classroom with a smudge of chalk dust on him somewhere. A chalkboard is readily available. It does not require extensive preparation. It can be used by both student and teacher. Here are 15 ways to use the chalkboard:

1. To introduce a new member or visitor
2. To highlight the memory verse
3. To outline or diagram the lesson points
4. To illustrate objects or ideas
5. To tell a story (using stick or cartoon figures)
6. To draw simple Bible maps
7. To record student comments and opinions
8. To show comparisons or contrasts
9. To conduct previews and reviews
10. To give a test or quiz
11. To make assignments or emphasize announcements
12. To define new words
13. To learn or make up a new song
14. To keep class records from week to week
15. To emphasize prayer requests

Flannelboard or Feltboard

This is one of the simplest pieces of visual aid available to any teacher. Materials may be quickly prepared. Ideas can be developed in sequence. Both the teacher and students can use the flannelboard. A flannelboard can be inexpensively made by taping, gluing, or stapling a piece of felt or flannel to a board. For this reason, it is possible to have several different size boards to fit various situations—small tabletop boards to use in the classroom or large boards mounted on an easel for use in an auditorium.

Use the flannelboard to tell a story, highlight lesson truths, aid memory. Involve the children by letting them place the pieces on the board as they review the lesson or story. Use the flannelboard as a map, using colored yarn to form waterways, boundaries, roadways, etc.

Use the flannelboard in youth and adult classes, too. Word strips of the lesson outline can be placed on it. Or it can be used as a bulletin board to display pictures, articles, announcements, etc.

Give the flannelboard a three-dimensional look by backing the figures with pieces of styrofoam or sponge. Make scenes look more realistic by pinning leaves, flowers, or bits of bark to the board. Create your own backgrounds using pieces of colored cloth or colored yarn. Use a fine wire brush to make an older board regain its holding power.

After you have prepared and used your figures, be sure to store them carefully for future use. Place the figures in a file folder or use a large magazine and place one figure on each page. File the figures by category with all the figures of people in one file or magazine, all the animal figures in another, and all the plants in still another. In this way you will be able to quickly find the materials to prepare a story.

Charts and Graphs

Youth and adults can quickly grasp information when shown on charts and graphs. The lesson outline can be put on a flip chart with a separate idea on each page. A large sketchpad can be used as a flip chart; several large sheets of paper can be held to a board with large spring clips. Several other types of charts are hanging charts, pocket charts, and rip charts.

Statistical information can be more easily analyzed when visualized on a line or bar graph. Use a time line to show the order of chronological events. Instruct the students to draw a line graph of their personal spiritual growth.

Several helpful principles to keep in mind when making charts, banners, and posters are: 1) Present one basic idea; 2) Keep it simple; 3) Organize the layout; 4) Create visual balance; 5) Be legible. It is best to use straight block print rather than an ornate style or script.

Maps and Globes

These can be widely used with all departments from primary through adult. Bible locations can be shown on flat maps. Use a globe to locate mission fields. Simple maps such as the one shown here can be drawn on the chalkboard or overhead projector. Pupils can make their own papier-mache maps when studying Bible geography.

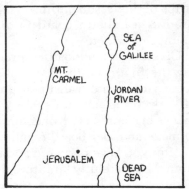

To store maps for ready reference, mount a small window shade on the classroom wall and tape or glue the maps to the shade. When not in use the shade can be rolled up.

Collages, Graffiti Posters, and Friezes

A *collage* is a collection of pictures or headlines cut from magazines by the students and glued on a piece of poster board to form a design or represent a theme.

A *graffiti poster* is a collection of writings, slogans, drawings, symbols, or cartoons done by the students on a piece of newsprint paper or poster board on a theme such as "Love is . . ."

A *frieze* is a series or sequence of pictures or cartoons by the students on a long piece of paper which tells a continuous story.

Other art projects which involve the students are mobiles, murals, advertisement brochures, bumper stickers, lapel buttons, etc. These activities provide creative ways for them to express the main emphasis of the lesson.

Sponge Painting

This technique is especially good for preschool children who sometimes find it difficult to draw within confined lines. Mix dry tempera paint and water to a thick consistency. Pour the paint into small containers or a muffin tin. Cut a soft sponge into small, irregular shapes. Attach a clip clothespin to each piece of sponge. Let the children dip the sponge into the paint and blot on white paper. They can create a variety of bright designs such as rainbows, flowers, etc. Have the children slip on an old adult-size shirt to protect their clothing when doing sponge painting or finger painting.

Tissue Lamination

This, too, is ideal for young children. Brush liquid starch on white paper. Let the children sprinkle torn pieces of tissue paper onto the wet starch. Then brush over the tissue paper with more liquid starch. The end result is a pretty mosaic effect as the colors in the tissue paper run and blend into each other. An older group of children could use this technique to make a stained-glass window design.

Creative Art Activities

Children enjoy easel painting. Tempera paints or water colors work best for this. Block tempera may be best for younger children since there is no chance of spilling. The children simply use a wet brush on the block of tempera color to make the paint.

Here are several ways to use those bits of broken crayon. Grind up several different crayons in a hand pencil sharpener. Let the children sprinkle the chips on white paper. Cover with wax paper and apply a hot iron. The heat causes the colors to melt together and creates a mosaic effect. Let the children color with a crayon on sandpaper. Then turn the sandpaper upside down onto white paper. Apply a hot iron to the backside of the sandpaper until the colors melt onto the bottom sheet. Make a multicolor crayon block by mixing ground crayon chips in small paper cups. Place the cups in a warm oven until the chips form a block. Remove from the oven and cool. The crayon block will create a multicolor effect on paper.

Puppets

Puppets can be made and used by both the teacher and pupils. More elaborate hand puppets can be made from a sock or fake fur. Use yarn for hair, buttons for eyes and nose, and red felt for the tongue. Children enjoy making paper bag puppets. The face is drawn on the bottom of the bag with the mouth placed where the edge of the bottom meets the side of the bag as shown. The students can make the mouth move by putting their hand inside the bag and moving their fingers. Puppets can be used to tell a Bible or life-application story, to direct group activities, to correct behavior, and so on. Children can make puppets of the characters of the Bible story and use them to retell the story.

Newspapers

Here is a visual aid every teacher has at his disposal, and it has a wealth of material for use in the classroom. Use the newspaper to relate Bible lessons to current issues. Have the students look for articles which illustrate how Christian principles compare with contemporary ethics. They might show how an editorial, a cartoon, or "Dear Abby" compares with what the Bible says. Look for news of other religions or cults. Study church ads and sermon topics. Collect articles about events in foreign countries where our missionaries are serving. Have the students clip and send articles of local news to military personnel or college students away from home. Use the want ad section as pages for a flip chart and write on them with a broad-tipped felt pen. The fine point cannot be seen from a distance.

PROJECTED VISUAL AIDS

Films and Filmstrips

Some of the various types of films and filmstrips available for rent or purchase are: missionary, evangelistic, leadership training, Bible story, science, documentary, and so on. These have many uses in Christian education, but they must be used correctly to be most effective. First of all, have a purpose for showing a film or filmstrip. It should never be used just as a time filler. Always preview the material before showing it to the group. Prepare the group for what they are going to see. Instruct them to look for key ideas or to note any questions the film or filmstrip may raise. Listening team assignments may be used. Have all the equipment set up properly beforehand. Practice using the projector if you are not familiar with it. After showing the film or filmstrip, give the class an opportunity to express their reactions to it. Ask them to recap what was said or call for reports from the listening teams. If you have time, you may want to show the film or filmstrip again to give the students opportunity to look for new insights or understandings.

Slides

There are several advantages to using slides. They can be produced locally to meet specific needs. The only cost is film and developing. Slides can be arranged in any order desired and they can be easily revised and updated. A slide presentation can be combined with narration to give an effective audiovisual impact.

Slides have many uses in teaching: 1) Show scenic slides to illustrate the wonders of God's creation. 2) Use slides to substitute for a class field trip. 3) Use slides to make the class aware of community needs. 4) Have someone take slides of class activities such as parties, projects, and so on, and use them to promote future activities. 5) Use slides in special programs such as Christmas or Easter programs to create backgrounds, decorations, special effects. 6) Purchase write-on slides from Kodak or make your own from matte finish acetate and slide mounts. Let the students write or draw on the slides and project them in the classroom. 7) Assign a class of youth or adults to prepare a slide presentation on a Biblical subject or a contemporary issue. 8) Have someone with a copying lens take slides of maps, charts, or other printed material. Use these as teaching aids. 9) Combine slides with music to illustrate a gospel song.

Overhead Projector

The overhead projector has been used for years in public education. Today it is being used more widely in the church. Pastors use it to illustrate Bible studies and sermons. Committees use it to visualize reports. Leaders use it to share plans. In the Sunday school superintendents are using it in worker's conferences, training sessions, planning meetings. And teachers are using the overhead projector to make their lessons come alive.

The overhead projector has several distinct advantages. 1) The teacher can face his students as he uses it. This enables him to maintain eye contact. 2) The overhead projector can be used in a fully or partially lighted room. 3) Transparency materials can be prepared ahead of time and preserved for future use. 4) By using overlays and masks the teacher can show progression of thought and keep the class from getting ahead of him. 5) Younger children can draw on the large transparency format.

Transparencies can be made in several ways. The teacher can draw directly on a clear sheet of acetate with a felt-tip pen or grease pencil. For more permanent transparencies transfer lettering may be used. Transparencies of printed material can be made on most office copying machines. Professional looking transparencies can be made using pressure sensitive color sheets, translucent tape, clear or tinted acetate, colored pens, etc. Many prepared transparencies are now available for purchase.

Transparencies can also be made using the color-lift process. To do this carefully apply adhesive-backed acetate to a picture. Rub out all the air bubbles. Then soak the acetate/paper sandwich in a pan of warm, soapy water until the paper becomes soft enough to slough off with gentle rubbing. This leaves the ink from the picture adhered to the acetate. Allow the acetate to air dry and coat the adhesive side with a clear plastic spray to protect it.

Some tips to remember in using the overhead projector are: 1) Project at an angle in the room so everyone can see around the instructor. 2) Position the screen as high as possible and keep the information on the transparency near to the top of the projection stage. 3) Be sure the projector is focused properly. 4) Point to the transparency on the projector stage rather than back to the image on the screen. 5) Do not walk between the projector and screen while the lamp is on. 6) Place the transparency on the stage before turning on the lamp. 7) Turn off the projector when you are not directly referring to what is being shown. 8) Keep your transparencies simple and uncluttered. Use no more than six or seven lines of copy. Use large, clear print.

AUDIO AIDS

Records

Records have many uses in the classroom. Children can sing along with records in departmental worship. Records can be used to set the mood in a classroom or assembly area. Play soft music before the worship time or lively music during activity times. Recorded music can be used to signal the change from one activity to another. Children can enjoy recorded music or stories in the listening center.

Records can also be used with youth and adults. Play an appropriate record as the students arrive in the classroom. Excerpts from contemporary music or speaking records can be used to spark class discussion. Records can also be given as awards or prizes.

Tape Recorder

The cassette recorder also has many uses in teaching. Many outstanding speakers can be brought to your classroom by way of the cassette recorder. When you do use recorded speakers keep the excerpt to no more than 5 or, at the most, 10 minutes. Follow up with a discussion of what was said. Use recorded sound effects to make stories more realistic. For an occasional change, play the Scripture portion from prerecorded Scripture tapes. Let the students use the tape recorder to assist them in Scripture memorization. Combine the tape recorder with headphones to create a listening center. Record your class sessions to evaluate your teaching. Use the tape recorder to prerecord the dialogue for skits and plays. Let the students write and record a dramatized Bible story or skit. Exchange cassettes with missionaries and their families. Use the tape recorder to share class sessions with absentees or shut-ins. Assign the students to interview several people outside of church and play the tape for the class. Tape radio or TV newscasts to highlight current events.

7 Preparing to Teach

Lord who am I to teach the way
* To little children day by day*
* So prone myself to go astray?*
I teach them knowledge, but I know
* How faint the flicker and how low*
* The candles of my knowledge glow.*
I teach them power to will and do
* But only now to learn anew*
* My own great weakness through and through.*
I teach them love for all mankind
* And all God's creatures, but I find*
* My love comes lagging far behind.*
Lord if their guide I still must be,
* Oh let the little children see*
* The teacher leaning hard on Thee.*

PREPARING THE HEART

This poem by Leslie Pincknew Hill expresses the way many of us feel about our role as teachers. We realize that we must first be ministered unto before we can expect to minister to others. In other words, we must prepare our own hearts and lives.

This involves, among other things, Bible study, prayer, and devotional reading. A teacher who wants to teach the written Word with effectiveness and with power must first speak to and be spoken to by the Living Word. He must be living in contact and fellowship with the Lord.

One of the greatest dangers for any Christian teacher is to feel that he is maintaining a devotional life when he goes through the routine of lesson study. Some may argue that they spend considerable time every week in lesson preparation and that additional devotional time is unnecessary. But this is not true. We do need to spend time with the Lord and His Word outside of our lesson study. As Lois LeBar has said, "The greatest competitor of devotion to Jesus is service for Him. . . . In order to bear more fruit upward, our roots have to go deeper down in the Lord. More than servants to work for Him, the Lord seeks sons to fellowship with Him." (Lois E. LeBar, *op. cit.*, p. 239.)

Bible Study

Some teachers study the Bible only to prepare for the coming lesson. This approach may add to their accumulation of Bible knowledge; but unfortunately, this often does not result in much spiritual development in the life of the teacher. Lesson study, however, can contribute to our devotional life if we guard against taking a strictly intellectual approach to the text and instead let the Scriptures first speak to us as a learner and not as a teacher. We must find in the Bible passage or story those truths that God has placed there for our personal growth.

The greatest threat to meaningful personal Bible study is to fall into a rut. It is wise to take a different approach to Bible study from that of lesson preparation. Occasionally try a topical or word study, or a historical or biographical study. Using different translations and paraphrases will add variety. Some of the new parallel text editions are excellent for comparing several different versions.

Have a pencil and paper handy and develop the habit of reacting to what you read. Outline or diagram the passage and list the key verses. Or make up a personal commentary as you read. Occasionally try writing your own paraphrase of the passage, putting the meaning of each verse into your own words. Keep these notes for future reference.

Prayer

The most common problems in many Christian's prayer life are: praying in generalities, limiting our prayer concerns, falling into a form or routine, and the problem of time. To overcome the problem of praying in generalities and also to expand your prayer life, try making a list of specific prayer needs you want to remember. Prepare a notebook with a page for each student in your class. Write down some of the needs each one has in his life. Refer to the notebook as you pray.

Occasionally use some different prayer forms in addition to spontaneous, extemporaneous prayer such as personally written prayers, prayers and litanies written by others, silent prayer and meditation, prayer songs and choruses, prayer poetry, and prayers from the Bible, such as those of David, Christ, Paul, and others.

Finding time for prayer and Bible study can be a problem. Here are several possibilities you may want to consider: 1) Early in the morning. Get dressed before you begin so you will be fully awake and alert. 2) Midmorning, after the family leaves for school and work. 3) At school or work during a break or study period. 4) After school or work. 5) Immediately after the evening meal. 6) At a different time on different days to meet a changing personal schedule. It will help you if you can have a specific place for devotions each day, a place to keep your devotional materials, a place somewhat away from the normal activities of the day.

Devotional Reading

"Give me a worker who reads" is the cry of leaders in every field. Every worker who takes his responsibility seriously, eagerly seizes upon every opportunity to improve himself in his field. The same should be true of Sunday school teachers. Reading offers numerous opportunities for spiritual growth and development. Bible knowledge is deepened, skills are sharpened, awareness of needs is heightened. Through reading we can associate with some of the great minds of the world.

A common lament of many people is that they do not have time to read. The answer may lie in taking advantage of brief moments of available time. A person who reads at normal speed for only 15 minutes each day will read 18 average-length books in 1 year. It is a good habit to carry a small paperback in your pocket or purse. Leave some good books around the house to read whenever a few minutes of time are available.

The next question is what to read? The vast number of books pouring from presses today make discrimination in reading necessary. One place to begin would be with periodicals. Our denomination publishes several excellent magazines, among them the *Pentecostal Evangel, Sunday School Counselor, SS Action,* and *Youth Alive.* Other good magazines are *Christian Life, Moody Monthly, Faith at Work, Home Life, and Christian Digest.*

Some of the more widely read inspirational authors today are Keith Miller, Bruce Larson, Rosalind Rinker, Francis Schaefer, Eugenia Price, Catherine Marshall, David Wilkerson, Pat Boone. Your local Christian bookstore stands ready to assist you with your reading needs. The Gospel Publishing House catalog also lists a broad choice of devotional, inspirational, and study books. The bibliography at the back of this book lists some of the outstanding works in the field of Christian education.

Read a variety of books. Reread books that have been particularly helpful. Again, read with a pencil in hand. Underline pertinent points; make notes in the margin.

PREPARING THE MIND

Lesson preparation begins several months in advance of the time the lesson is taught in class, or at least it should. The teacher should be familiar with the entire series of lessons in the curriculum cycle. He should start each new quarter by reading quickly through the entire teacher's manual in one sitting if possible. This will help him to see how each lesson fits into the whole. He can also begin to collect teaching materials to use in coming lessons.

Scripture Study

Specific lesson study begins with a thorough study of the Bible story or passage. As you read, look for the central truth, order of events, comparisons, contrasts, development of ideas, and so on. Six interrogative questions you might use are: *Who* are the persons involved? *Where* are the locations and settings referred to? *When* did the events occur? *How* are the facts presented? *Why* did things happen as they did or why did the author say what he did? *What* is the relevance of the story or passage to us today?

Read the passage or story in several versions. Consult a Bible dictionary, concordance, Bible handbook, or commentary. Study the context and historical setting. Let the passage speak to your own life and make notes of your thoughts and impressions.

Quarterly Study

Preparation also includes a careful study of curriculum materials. The teacher should read the material in the student quarterly as well as in his own teacher's quarterly. He should make note of questions which are raised and jot down ideas for teaching methods, pupil activities, illustrations, lesson introduction, and application. Throughout his preliminary preparation the teacher should be thinking of the lesson in terms of his pupils' needs and how this truth would apply to their lives.

Using Curriculum

This might be the appropriate place to say a word about the purpose and use of curriculum. A good Sunday school curriculum does serve several valuable purposes. It provides a systematic study with balance and comprehensiveness. All curriculum publishers work on a "building block" theory of organization in which the material for each age-level is based on what precedes it and prepares the way for what follows. The problem is that not all publishers use the same system. This is why it is not wise to order materials from several different sources.

A good curriculum provides a graded study. Curriculum writers are specialists in the age-group with which they work and take into account the needs, interests, and capabilities of the students at different stages of development. Some Bible stories or passages would be too difficult for younger children to understand.

Curriculum provides educationally sound design and organization of methods and materials. Bible portions are taught in proper sequence. The latest teaching techniques and learning activities can be incorporated. A balanced lesson plan is provided.

Word of Life curriculum from the Gospel Publishing House serves these purposes and more. The most important benefit of our curriculum is that it is Biblically accurate and doctrinally complete. The materials are checked frequently to be sure they are true to the Bible. And all the curriculum is written by Spirit-filled writers and editors, so they reflect the Pentecostal viewpoint of scriptural interpretation, theology, history, ethics, and so on. These materials are then taught by Spirit-filled teachers to Spirit-filled students. Thus the common experience of the infilling of the Holy Spirit underlies the teaching/learning process from beginning to end. It could be said, "If you want to produce good Baptists, use a Baptist curriculum. If you want to produce students with a liberal inclination, use a liberal curriculum. But if you want to produce Pentecostal students, use a Pentecostal curriculum."

One further reason for using Word of Life curriculum is that the Gospel Publishing House is *your* publishing house. The operation is owned by and controlled by the Assemblies of God. When you purchase materials from the Gospel Publishing House you are making an investment in the ministries of the Fellowship. Profits from other publishers may go to the owners or stockholders, to lavish promotions, and so on. Gospel Publishing House funds go directly into the work of the Assemblies of God.

But to be effective curriculum must be properly used. Two common errors in using curriculum are to follow it too closely or not closely enough. One teacher may practically read his lesson to the class from its pages. Another may ignore it and develop his own materials, usually on a favorite topic or two. The fact is the curriculum is a guide, not a slavemaster. It should be used as a tool to aid the teacher in his study and development of the lesson.

No curriculum publisher can produce lessons that will exactly fit every local situation and need. Usually the quarterly gives more material than can be used in a single session. The job of the teacher, then, is to decide which parts of the lesson best meet the needs of his students and adapt the lesson materials to fit those needs. A good teacher will construct a personal lesson plan, drawing on material from his own study of the Bible, the quarterly, and other sources.

PREPARING THE CLASSROOM

Teachers are constantly urged to spend more time in lesson preparation, to use a variety of teaching methods, and so on. Yet one of the most important factors in the teaching/learning process is often ignored. Next to the personality of the teacher, the classroom environment is the most important influence on the pupil. The best trained teacher, using the latest techniques and materials, will not be totally effective if the environment is not conducive to learning. *Where* the pupil learns has much to do with *what* and *how* he learns.

The learning environment is important for these reasons:

1. It is a continual source of instruction. The classroom begins to teach the moment the first student arrives, and its impressions are retained long after he leaves.

2. The appearance of his room tells the student much about the attitude of his teacher toward him and toward his or her responsibility as a teacher.

3. The room reflects the subject matter being taught. And unfortunately in some situations the surroundings speak so loudly the pupils cannot hear what the teacher is saying.

So preparation and maintenance of the classroom, then, are an important part of the teacher's responsibility. But what are some things the teacher should consider in preparing his classroom or department area?

Light

Since we learn more by sight than by any other sense, the quality of lighting in the room is very important. Check to see that there is enough light and that it is properly distributed throughout the room. You should also have some way to control the amount of light to meet different needs such as semidarkness for projected visuals, soft light for worship activities, and bright light for reading and handwork. Window shades and a dimmer switch can help achieve this control. Also be sure to seat the students away from or to the side of any natural light coming into the room.

Decoration

The decorating scheme in your room has a great influence on the mental and emotional attitudes of your students. Colors like orange, red, or yellow give a feeling of warmth, but they tend to make a room feel smaller. Blues and greens create a more relaxed, cool atmosphere and make a room appear larger. Bright color accents should be limited to bulletin boards and interest centers. A long, hard-to-light hallway should be painted a light color. The walls in the children's departments should be bright and cheery; the wall covering or paint, durable and scrubbable. Floor coverings of vinyl or commercial grade carpet should be chosen for ease of frequent and thorough cleaning. A bulky storage cabinet in a small room can be made less obvious by painting it the same color as the walls. An old piano can be painted to harmonize with the room decor and its back covered with a tack board. In this way it can be pulled out from the wall to serve as a room divider and also provide additional display space.

Furnishings

The physical comfort of the students is an important responsibility of the teacher. Tables and chairs should be the right size for the age-group. Also be sure there is a chair for everyone in the room plus a few extra for visitors. Keep all furnishings in good repair with an occasional refinishing or painting job. Select tables with adjustable folding legs when purchasing new equipment. In the long run it is usually better to buy high quality furnishings rather than cheaper, more poorly made goods. The type of furnishings purchased by public schools are often best for the church and Sunday school too.

Check to see that chalkboards, bulletin boards, tack rails, and so on are mounted at eye level and keep displays and bulletin boards current. Also provide ample storage space for learning resources, audiovisual equipment, teaching supplies, craft materials, and so on. Provide open shelves for the children to use in putting away supplies and closed, lockable cabinets for the workers.

Ventilation

Good ventilation and maintenance of even temperature are important if the students are to remain attentive and alert. The heating and cooling system should keep temperatures for each classroom within the comfort range throughout the class period and at all levels of capacity. Learning and attention are stimulated when the temperature is just slightly on the cool side. Floors in the preschool rooms must be kept warm and draft free.

Maintenance

The atmosphere of a room is often determined by its general appearance and maintenance. The furnishings in the classroom should be neatly arranged before the students begin to arrive. The floor, walls, and ceiling should be clean and in good repair, the windows and corners free of cobwebs and dust, the curtains clean and properly hung. Try to keep papers and teaching materials from accumulating on tables, counters, and atop the piano. Storage cabinets should be cleaned and rearranged frequently. Drinking fountains should be free of debris, rest rooms clean and adequately supplied.

Does all this mean your church should immediately launch into an extensive remodeling project or building program? Well, that may eventually be necessary, but in the meantime there is much that can be done to improve the present facilities:

1. Begin by taking a survey of your facilities. The leaders could evaluate the rooms and assembly areas in their department. Or the teachers could evaluate their own rooms and make a list of needed improvements.

2. Plan a work day. Get the staff or students together for a work day. This could be on an individual department basis or as an all-school project. Plan ahead by making a list of desired improvements and securing needed supplies in advance.

3. Preserve the floorspace in your room. This is where learning activities take place. If your room is small, remove the tables and use lapboards for writing and drawing. Replace bulky storage cabinets with hanging wall units. Or place storage cabinets outside of the classroom area.

4. Use folding partitions to subdivide large areas into individual classes or interest centers. Bookcases and storage shelves can also be used as dividers.

5. The best way to secure needed improvements and purchases is to make them a part of your annual Sunday school budget. Teachers should have opportunity to suggest needed purchases and improvements. Older classes or a group of teachers may want to conduct a special fund drive to raise money for a particular item needed in their class or department. People in the church may donate needed equipment or give money for special projects.

8 Steps of Lesson Planning

Okay, so the teacher has a basic understanding of the teaching/learning process and his role as a teacher. He knows and loves his students and he uses methods that involve them in the learning process. He has prepared his heart and mind as best he knows how. Now how does he go about putting everything together in a lesson plan that really teaches and that results in real learning?

STRUCTURING THE LESSON AIM

"The reason some folks don't git no whar is that they wun't goin' no whar in the fust place," said the country philosopher. The same thing could be said of many Sunday school teachers—their teaching is aimless. Too often little is learned and little happens because the teacher is not sure what he wanted the class to learn or what he wanted to have happen.

Many teachers spend time studying their lessons, constructing a lesson plan, collecting teaching materials, and planning their methods but fail to write out a lesson aim. Communicating the Word of God is too important to be left to such aimless teaching. If every teacher would structure a good lesson aim, that one thing would probably do more to improve the quality of Christian education in the local church than anything else.

What Is a Lesson Aim?

The dictionary defines an aim as "activity directed in an

orderly manner toward the realization of some end." In Sunday school teaching the aim is simply a statement of that which the teacher desires to have happen in the life of the students as a result of the lesson study. The aim may be expressed as a direct statement: "To help each student to discover areas of his life in which he may be limiting Christ and to begin to yield to Him in those areas." Or the aim may be expressed in the form of a question from the student which the lesson study would seek to answer: "What are some areas of my life in which I may be limiting Christ? How can I begin to yield to Him in these areas?"

There are several different types of aims:

The ultimate aim. The apostle Paul gave us our goal as Christian educators in Ephesians 4:13: "Till we all come in the unity of the faith, and of the knowledge of the Son of God, unto a perfect man, unto the measure of the stature of the fullness of Christ." Or to restate it, our ultimate objective is to see our students grow toward full maturity in Christ—at every age and in every way to be growing to be like Him.

Quarterly and unit aims. The ultimate aim (which, of course, is a life-long goal) will only be achieved in part and then only through a series of shorter, more intermediate aims. These are the quarterly and unit aims. It is important, then, that each teacher formulate an aim for the entire series of lessons in the quarter. This will help him to see how each lesson fits into the whole. The quarterly aim is then divided into several unit aims covering two or more lessons that go together.

Lesson aims. The individual lesson aims are the immediate steps taken toward the accomplishment of the unit and quarterly aims.

Educators often speak of three kinds of lesson aims: 1) Knowledge aims; 2) Attitude aims; and 3) Conduct aims. They correspond to the levels of learning discussed in chapter 3. A good lesson aim will usually include elements of all three, although one may be singled out for special emphasis.

However, if our overall goal is growth toward maturity in

Christ, teaching with a content or knowledge aim alone will not achieve it. Nor will an aim that focuses only on attitudes or inspiration. To teach for growth we must teach for conduct response. To *know* and to *feel* are part of the response to *do*. Response is preceded by a change of knowledge and a change of attitude. A needed emphasis in Sunday school teaching is teaching for a change in conduct and behavior.

Why Is a Lesson Aim Needed?

The very nature of learning makes lesson aims necessary. Learning is usually not an activity engaged in for its own sake. It is a means to an end. Take for example a teenager learning to drive a car. He doesn't study the "Rules of the Road" manual just so he can say he has mastered its contents. He doesn't take the driver's test just so he can tell his friends he has passed. He does all this so he can get his license and hit the road. Learning to drive is only a means to an end.

Christian education, too, is a means to an end. The final goal is maturity in Christ. Each lesson is a step in that direction—a change, a response that brings the learner closer to conformity to the image of Christ.

If this is the case, then, before the teacher can make plans for learning to take place, he must have clearly in mind the ends to be attained. The teacher must decide where he is going before he can plan how he will get there. The clearer the aim, the easier it will be to plan for its attainment.

We can see something more about the need for an aim by looking at some of the consequences of a lack of lesson aims. Without a lesson aim the teacher may try to cover too much material. Aimless teaching tends to ramble. Lessons taught without an aim are often unrelated to pupils' life-needs. Without a clear focus on response, teaching usually results in little change.

What Is the Purpose of a Lesson Aim?

Good teaching aims serve these four important functions:

1. Lesson aims serve as the major controlling factor in the teaching/learning process.

2. Lesson aims give proper sequence to the class activities and assure continuity and order in progression toward the goal.

3. Lesson aims serve as a guide in the selection of methods and materials. Some parts of the curriculum are left out, others are enlarged upon. Some methods are used, others are not. All of these decisions are made on the basis of the lesson aim.

4. Lesson aims serve as a basis for evaluation. "Did the methods we used help us reach our goal? Did we include the right materials? Did we see a change in our students?" These are questions the aim can help to answer. The accomplishment of stated aims brings a sense of satisfaction to both the teacher and the learner.

What Are the Qualities of a Good Lesson Aim?

A good lesson aim has these characteristics:

1. It must be concise enough to be written down. It is not enough to have a lesson aim in the back of your mind. You must be able to write it out briefly and clearly, in a single sentence if possible. Only then can it guide your lesson development.

2. It must be specific enough to be attainable. Most lesson aims are too broad and too general. To accept a general principle does not mean that principle will automatically operate in all areas of our lives. The lesson aim seeks to suggest specific areas in the life of the pupil in which the Biblical principle can be put into practice. The response called for must be realistic enough to be achieved by the learner in the coming weeks.

3. It must be flexible enough to be personalized. It is possible to make a lesson aim too specific. No teacher can know all the areas of need in the lives of his students, so the lesson aim must be flexible enough to permit the Holy Spirit to guide each learner to the unique response He chooses for him to make.

How Do I Select a Lesson Aim?

This is the most difficult and yet most important part of lesson planning. Two factors must be considered in choosing the lesson aim: First, the aim must grow out of the meaning of the Bible passage or story. It is never legitimate to "read into" a passage or story what it does not say. The aim should always be based on sound principles of Bible study and interpretation. Second, the aim must be related to the needs of the members of the class. This, of course, means the teacher must know the needs of his students. Once the teacher sees where the lesson truth touches on the life-needs of his students, he has practically arrived at the formulation of his lesson aim.

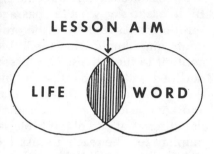

"But what about the aim printed in the curriculum materials? Can't we just use it as our lesson aim?" No curriculum writer could begin to structure an aim that would meet the needs of all the groups of students that use his materials. The suggested aim will help, but usually the teacher will have to restate the aim according to the unique needs of his class.

PREPARING THE LESSON PLAN

After structuring the lesson aim, the teacher must develop a lesson plan that will help him accomplish that aim. The following four-step plan is suggested:

Lesson approach. The first few minutes of the class are most important in terms of student interest. If you do not capture the attention and interest of your students in the opening moments, you may lose them for the entire period. So you must carefully plan a good approach to the lesson.

The lesson approach should do three things: It should arouse interest, involve the students, and lead naturally into the lesson study. The students should be made ready to discover Biblical answers to their personal needs. To do this the teacher may pose a problem or raise a question which will be answered in the lesson. Some of the methods to use in introducing the lesson are: life-situation stories, open-ended stories, current events, brainstorming, agree-disagree questions, skits, roleplays, or interviews.

Bible content. Here our concern is to understand what the Bible has to say, what the passage or story is all about, what solution it has to offer to the problem or situation. Our students must know what the Bible teaches before they can apply it to their lives. The lesson material must be clearly outlined with the main points supported and reinforced; or the story must be outlined as to introduction, body, climax, and conclusion. The lesson aim will guide the teacher in deciding what part of the Bible story or Scripture passage to emphasize. The teacher must decide what additional materials will be used such as other Bible stories, illustrations, current events, visual aids, and so on. Methods used in developing the Bible content may include symposiums, panels, group Bible studies, listening teams, Bible drama, research projects.

Personalizing the lesson. In this section of the lesson plan the teacher attempts to help the students to see the implications of the spiritual truth for their personal lives. It is not enough to know what the Bible says. The students must be led to see situations in their lives in which this truth would apply. They must be guided to focus on specific areas of personal need. The most frequently used method to accomplish this is to use good thought-provoking questions. Other methods might include personal questionnaires, self-evaluations, case studies, art or writing projects, buzz groups, circle response.

Applying the lesson. It is not enough to know Bible truth or even to see its implications for life. The teacher must go to the last step and help the students actually begin to apply the lesson truth in their lives. Here is where the lesson aim is actually carried out. This part of the lesson must not be left up to a spur-of-the-moment thought as the class period ends but must be carefully planned in advance. Class members must be led to come to their own conclusions, guided by the gentle proddings of the teacher. The class should decide on specific steps they will take to begin to respond to the lesson truth in their lives. The process must be unhurried, so enough time must be allowed for it. Some of the methods used may be written reminders, individualized and group projects, prayer and share groups, keeping a log or diary, and so on. The teacher should also plan how he will follow up on the students during the week and next Sunday, such as with a phone call, card, group reports, or personal conversation.

Writing Out the Lesson Plan

This is what the teacher will take into the classroom; so it should include everything he will need to teach the lesson. Every teacher will develop his own style at this point. It may be a manuscript, sentence, phrase, or word outline. At any rate it should include the four basic elements discussed above. It is usually best not to teach directly from the quarterly.

The teacher must also think through the amount of time needed for each part of the lesson. The time schedule should then be written somewhere on the lesson plan, possibly on the left-hand margin.

A Sample Lesson Plan

Here is how a lesson plan from Amos 1 and 2 might be developed for a group of teachers using the pattern suggested above:

Lesson Aim: That each worker will ask God to point out unrecognized sin in his life.

(5 min.)

Lesson Approach: Help me with a problem. A young pastor noticed that one of his teachers is falling down in several areas of his life. As you would expect, the pastor is concerned but somewhat hesitant to speak to him. He wants to do it in just the right way. How should he approach the teacher? (Have them divide into small groups and discuss and write out an approach.)

(15 min.)

Bible Content: While they are still in their buzz groups say: "Amos was a backhills shepherd sent by God to take a message to the wealthy, complacent people of power in Israel. Turn in your Bible to the first two chapters of his book and let's find out how Amos approached these people with the message God gave him." (Uncover flip chart saying, "How did he introduce his message?" Allow about 5 minutes for them to answer these questions which you will write on a flip chart or overhead projector: 1) What sort of a message was it? 2) To whom was he speaking? 3) Where did he begin, what countries did he mention?)

After discussion in buzz groups, write their answers to the first two questions on the flip chart or overhead projector. Then locate on a map the countries mentioned in answer to the third question. (Uncover this question on the flip chart: Why did he lead up to the message in this way?) Ask: "What would have happened if he had begun immediately with 'For three transgressions of Israel, and for four . . . ,' how would you expect proud, prosperous, complacent people to react? What sort of reaction would Amos have received from the people of Israel at the denunciation of their enemies? After they had agreed seven times about the justice of God's judgment for sin, could they then deny their own guilt?"

(20 min.)

Application: If Amos were sent by God today, would he have to begin by bringing up such topics as Portugal, Angola, the Middle East, governmental scandal, a rising crime rate (show newspaper clippings with such headlines), or could he say right here in (your town), "Sunday school teacher, there are some things in your life which are not pleasing to me—if they are not taken away, judgment is inevitable"? Are we satisfied with our present state, or do we ask God to show us unrecognized sin so we may get rid of it? Let's silently ask Him to do this right now. (Silent prayer for a few moments.)

In what areas are Sunday school teachers particularly susceptible to secret sin? (Pass out 3 x 5 cards and have them list these.) Keep asking specific questions until you get each person to narrow down to one or two specific personal needs.

Have each one write on this card what he could begin to do about his need. Ask each one to put the card in his Bible or someplace where he will see it again this week. Send them home with this heart-searching attitude by reading together Psalm 139:23, 24, "Search me, O God. . . ."

SECURING LESSON APPLICATION

Most Sunday school teachers do a reasonably good job of teaching basic Bible content. It is at the applicational level that they need help. How do some teachers approach the matter of lesson application? Let's talk to a few:

"I just teach the lesson content and let the pupils make their own application. I believe that if the truth is presented clearly, the pupils will automatically put it into practice."

"I always try to close each lesson with a story that illustrates how someone else applied the lesson truth in his life. I feel that if the students see how others responded to the Biblical truth, they will want to do the same."

"I always encourage my pupils to apply the lesson truth in the coming week by closing with a few general suggestions for them to follow."

None of these three approaches to application is really adequate. The first often results in little actual change in the lives of the pupils because lesson truths do not automatically transfer from knowledge to practice. The second is somewhat better, but it often works only if a situation arises in the pupils' lives very similar to the one that was illustrated in class. The third approach is not specific enough, since it does not help the pupils plan how to apply the lesson principles in their lives.

A widely accepted definition of teaching and learning states: "The teacher has not taught until the pupil has learned, and the pupil has not learned until he is putting into practice that which he has been taught." So how do we develop a lesson plan that results in that kind of teaching and learning? In the preceding unit of this chapter we divided the lesson application into two steps. Let's look at them more closely at this time.

In his book, *Creative Bible Teaching,* Lawrence Richards suggests an approach to lesson application called "Guided Self-Application." (Lawrence Richards, *op. cit.,* pp. 119-126.) This approach involves the following five steps:

1. The pupils are led to restate the Biblical principle in their own words.

2. The pupils are guided to see several areas of their lives in which the principle applies.

3. The pupils are led to narrow these down to one area for deeper exploration.

4. The pupils are guided to think through in depth the implications of the Biblical truth in this one area of their lives.

5. The pupils are led to plan how to act upon the truth and are encouraged to do what they have planned.

In this process the teacher acts as a guide, but the pupils are led to make their own application. Thus it is more personal, is remembered longer, and is more likely to be acted upon. Also the pupils learn for themselves how to apply Biblical truths—a skill they can use later in their personal Bible study.

Sample Lesson Application

Let's see how "Guided Self-Application" could work with a class of primaries studying a lesson on the Good Samaritan. We'll number the parts of the plan to correspond with the five steps of the "Guided Self-Application" approach.

1. The class could replay the story with different children playing the parts of the people in the story. This will determine if everyone understands the details of the parable.

2. Ask: "Who are some people that it's sometimes hard to be kind to?" Their replies may include the following: brother, sister, grouchy neighbor, bully, new kid, someone who's different, etc.

3. Distribute paper and crayons. Ask each student to draw a picture of a person that it's sometimes hard to be kind to.

4. Talk about ways we could show these people kindness like the good Samaritan did. Ideas may include: help them, share with them, smile.

5. Ask the children to draw a picture on the other side of the paper of something they will do this week to show kindness to the person it's hard for them to be kind to. Have them take the paper home where it will remind them of what they said they would do. Next Sunday ask them what happened when they tried to show kindness.

Here's a simple lesson for a group of teachers based on 2 Timothy 2:15:

1. Distribute paper and pencils. Ask each person to write a personal paraphrase of the verse, putting its meaning into his own words.

2. Divide the teachers into small groups. Instruct them to discuss ways they as teachers should obey this verse in their personal Bible study and lesson preparation. Call for reports from the groups. List their comments on the left side of the chalkboard as shown in box on next page.

3. Ask the teachers to write down one thing they could each do to improve their Bible study and lesson preparation. They can draw from the list on the chalkboard. Write the

Pray before studying	List student prayer needs.
	Pray for each student by name.
Regular time for study	Begin study on Monday.
	Set up schedule for the week.
Read lesson context	Look up parallel passages.
	Read entire chapter or chapters.
Use study helps	Use concordance, dictionary.
	Purchase study helps.

following questions on a flip chart and lead the teachers in a general discussion: "What can we do to begin to act upon these principles of Bible study?" List these ideas on the right side of the chalkboard opposite each of the general principles as shown above.

4. Instruct the teachers to write down three specific things they will try to do this week to act on the area they indicated needed improvement in their study.

5. Ask each person to turn to the one sitting next to him and explain what he will do to improve his Bible study and lesson preparation. Close with each person praying for the one next to him.

In Summary

It is absolutely necessary that we think of our teaching in terms of securing lesson application and response from our pupils. If our students get used to discovering Biblical truths without doing anything about them, they are forming disastrous habits. As teachers we must guide the pupils to apply Biblical truths in their lives during the class. And we must also help them during the week. If we teach in this manner, we will certainly see results as our pupils grow toward real maturity in Christ.

9 Evaluating Your Teaching

Evaluation is a normal part of our everyday lives. We engage in it constantly—when we choose one product over another or when we taste a cake someone has baked. We evaluate our friends, our boss, the weatherman, the newspaper we read, the television programs we watch. And we depend on evaluation to ensure our safety and well-being. We would not use a product that we thought was not properly tested. We would not fly in an airplane that was not thoroughly inspected before each trip. We would not go to a doctor who had not completed his training and been properly examined.

And yet some Sunday school teachers resist any effort to evaluate themselves or have anyone else evaluate their work. To fail to evaluate our efforts is as illogical as using an untested drug or flying in an unsafe airplane. When we do not evaluate ourselves, we tend to keep making the same mistakes over and over again. We become stuck in a rut with a resulting decrease in effectiveness and a loss of enthusiasm both from ourselves and our students.

The fact is our teaching is constantly being evaluated by others whether we are aware of it or not. It is being tested by our pupils, by their parents, by other teachers, by life itself. and most important by God himself.

Until a few years ago, little emphasis was placed upon what was actually accomplished through Sunday school teaching. Everyone seemed to think that it was sufficient that the pupils were physically present in the class. Whether they really learned anything was almost incidental. But then someone began to question the validity of the Sunday school. Articles in leading magazines called it the most wasted hour of the week. Others predicted its soon demise. And so we face a somewhat different situation regarding the Sunday school today. Its place as the principal outreach and teaching ministry of the church has been reaffirmed. But today people expect results; they want something to happen in Sunday school. It is essential, then, that we evaluate our teaching ministries to make sure that we are accomplishing what is expected of us.

What do we mean by evaluation? According to the dictionary, when you evaluate anything you make an appraisal of its merits or value. To evaluate means to review or measure an existing situation or to compare it with accepted practices or goals. In Sunday school teaching evaluation involves examining the teaching/learning process for the purpose of improving its effectiveness.

What is the need for and purpose of evaluation? Findley Edge suggests several important needs for testing and evaluation. (Findley Edge, *op. cit.*, pp. 175, 176.) 1) The seriousness of our task demands accurate evaluation. As Christian teachers we are dealing with eternal truth and eternal destinies. We must know if we are getting the job done. 2) The startling lack of Bible knowledge requires that we evaluate what we are doing. Tests continue to reveal that students often learn pathetically little even though they have attended Sunday school for years.

Evaluation serves these important purposes:

1. It gives the teacher a self-profile by helping him answer the question: "What kind of a teacher am I?"

2. Evaluation is the first step toward improvement. Before he can know what he needs to do, he must know what he is doing now.

3. Evaluation can help to identify the problem areas so the teacher can work on these weaknesses.

4. Evaluation can also help to rekindle the teacher's zeal for teaching as he analyzes his strengths as well as his weak-

nesses, his successes as well as his failures. It is nice to know what is working as well as what is not.

5. Self-appraisal can help the teacher set goals for the future. As he sees what he is doing, he can plan for what he would like to be doing.

6. Testing and evaluation can stimulate greater learning. As the students come to realize that they will be asked to account for what they have been taught, they may become more involved in the learning experience. As someone has said: "You get what you inspect, not what you expect."

7. Evaluation can encourage parent-home cooperation. As the teacher discusses the pupil's progress with his parents, they may become more involved in assuming their responsibility of providing spiritual training in the home.

8. Evaluation can strengthen the ministry of the entire Sunday school. The best way to improve the Sunday school is to improve the staff. Regular evaluations can motivate that improvement among all the workers, or at least, point out those who are willing to improve.

What should you evaluate? Guy Leavitt suggests we compare this to a housewife evaluating a cake she has baked. (*Teach With Success* [Cincinnati: Standard Publishing, 1956], p. 126.) She first wants to know how it tasted to those who ate it. Did they like it? What did they say? Did they ask for another piece? She can tell a lot about her cake by how it was received by others. Then she may ask herself about the ingredients: What went into the cake? Were they of good quality? Did she use the right amounts? Did she mix them thoroughly? Was the oven temperature correct? What could she do to make a better cake next time?

The Sunday school teacher asks some of the same questions about his teaching. His first concern should be for the students. What did they learn? Did they enjoy the classroom experience? Did they come back for more? Then he may consider the ingredients of his teaching. Did he use the best methods? Were the materials appropriate to the aim? Did the lesson plan work? Did he spend enough time in preparation? What could he have done differently or better?

We will look at each of these aspects of evaluation in more detail—the pupil, the lesson, and the teacher.

EVALUATING YOUR PUPILS

If the pupil is the focal point of Sunday school teaching, then evaluation must begin with him. We must be conscious of the results of our teaching as it affects our pupils. Our evaluation of the pupils' progress is an essential part of the teaching/learning process. It is just as necessary as thorough lesson preparation or effective presentation. A system of evaluation helps the teacher to know the learner's ability, knowledge, skills, attitude, interests, and behavior. The teacher needs to know where his pupils are so he can devise a way to take them where they need to be. He needs to know their interests so he can associate their interests with the material he is presenting. He needs to know their abilities and needs so he can counsel and guide them. The teacher must know how his pupils are progressing in order to determine the direction of their future study.

At times it is difficult to really determine the results of your teaching in the lives of your pupils. This is because spiritual growth is an inner process. The results cannot be determined with a tape measure or scale. A test of Bible knowledge does not always indicate the pupil's internal acceptance and response to that knowledge. The measurement of spiritual progress is often more a matter of subjective opinion than objective fact. So this means the teacher must not jump to conclusions based on what may be inadequate information, but must consider all the evidence and remain open-minded.

Evaluation is further complicated by the fact that pupils enter our class with a wide range of backgrounds and experiences. What may be acceptable to one may be unacceptable to another. So it is not always easy to determine just what each pupil is actually supposed to know, feel, or be able to do at the conclusion of a class session. This points up that our evaluation must be on an individual basis.

Some pupils may feel threatened by evaluation. So the teacher must be careful to explain that he is not merely checking up on his students, but is fulfilling his responsibility as a teacher.

While numbers can give some indication of a teacher's success, they may not tell all the story. Just because a class is growing or declining does not necessarily mean it is the result of good or bad teaching. The teacher must try to get the whole story.

In spite of these difficulties, a reasonably accurate evaluation of your teaching as it relates to your students is possible. But it requires time and effort on your part. Learning is a continuous process; so evaluation, too, must be a continuous effort—not just periodically but week to week. A good teacher must be constantly looking for new and better ways to test the progress of his pupils.

What Aspects of Your Pupils' Progress Should You Consider?

The teacher should ask himself these questions regarding each student's *relationship to Christ:* Does he appear to understand the plan of salvation? Has he accepted Christ as his personal Saviour? Has he been baptized in water? In the Holy Spirit? How does he evidence that his life is committed to Christ?

Areas to consider regarding the pupil's *spiritual growth* may include: Does he engage in Bible study outside of class? Does he have a time of personal devotions? Is he applying Biblical truths in his life? Is he developing a Christian lifestyle? Is he sharing his faith in Christ with others? Is he learning to be a good steward of his resources, time, abilities, and so on?

Questions to ask regarding the pupil's *church involvement* are: Is the pupil faithful in his attendance at Sunday school and church? Does he seem to enjoy these activities? Does he take part in out-of-class activities? Does he bring his friends to Sunday school and church? Is he assuming class and church responsibilities? Does he speak well of the class and church?

Regarding the pupil's *Bible and doctrinal knowledge* you should ask: Does he have an adequate understanding of the Bible for his age? Can he explain the basic doctrines of salvation, healing, Baptism, and second coming? Is he growing in his Bible study skills?

Change in the pupil's *attitude and actions* are often difficult to determine, but the teacher must know how much teaching is actually being translated into action in the lives of the pupils. So he will be continually looking for evidences of growth in these hard-to-measure areas—attitude and response toward God, the church, other Christians, missions, Christian standards, and so on.

Ways to Test Your Pupils

Observation. A teacher can determine to a great extent the response of his pupils to his teaching by careful observation. Much can be learned about the pupil's spiritual growth and church involvement in this way.

Pupil data sheet. Many of the questions raised above could be used to create a pupil data sheet. This form could be filled out by the teacher, the pupil, or his parents. A teacher-pupil or teacher-parent conference could be set up for this purpose.

Tests. Various kinds of tests can be devised to determine the pupil's understanding of Bible knowledge and doctrine such as true-false, matching, completion, multiple choice, and oral tests. Essays have the advantage of requiring the student to think through his answer and express it in his own words. The study questions in the lesson materials can be used to compile a test. The pupils may be assigned to answer a set of questions based on each lesson. Questions that would help determine attitudes and responses could be included along with factual questions. A quiz could be given at the beginning and end of a quarter to determine what information the pupils have learned.

The finished product of the Christian teacher is a student who is growing toward spiritual maturity. No conscientious teacher will be satisfied with his teaching until he knows that his students have found Christ, that they are Spirit-filled, that they are growing in the understanding of the Word, and that they are stable, fruit-bearing Christians. Student testing helps him determine this information.

EVALUATING YOUR PRESENTATION

The pupil's success or failure in learning is largely a result of the teacher's success or failure in teaching. So evaluation must include your lesson presentation in the classroom, your conducting of the teaching/learning situation. IIere again there are several important areas to consider.

Watch Your Appearance

Poise and self-confidence are necessary for an effective lesson presentation, and your appearance has much to do with how you feel about yourself in the classroom. Your students consciously or unconsciously size you up and pass judgment on you every time you appear before them. So take time to prepare physically. Be sure your clothes are neat and well-fitting; but, do not dress to attract undue attention to yourself. Arriving in the classroom ahead of your students will also help to give you greater self-confidence.

Your posture and teaching position can affect your presentation. With young children it may be best to sit with them on the story rug or on a low chair or stool. The important thing is to be at eye level with your pupils. Also remember to hold any objects such as pictures or models at eye level. It is a good idea with youth and adults to vary your position occasionally. Change from sitting to standing. When you stand, stand tall—give the class your full stature. Whenever possible, try to join the class at a table or in a circle.

Learn to use a few natural gestures and facial expressions.

Let your body reinforce your words, and your whole teaching manner will be more effective. Your effectiveness will also be enhanced by maintaining eye contact with your class. Try to correct bad habits such as looking at the floor or ceiling, looking out a window, or only looking at one or two students.

Watch Your Attitude

The attitude of the teacher becomes the attitude of the class. A teacher who is uptight soon makes his students feel the same way. On the other hand, a teacher who is relaxed soon puts his students at ease too. Work at making your students feel comfortable in your class or department.

Be cheerful and positive. The classroom is not the place to parade your woes or air your "pet peeves." Cultivate a warm, friendly atmosphere. Be open toward different ideas. Be a good listener—listen for hidden meanings behind your students' words. Concentrate on what they are saying and not on what you are going to say in reply.

Be enthusiastic. You'll find that it's very contagious. Let your love for the Lord, for His Word, and for your students show on your face, in your words, by your attitudes, through your actions. Be alive and your class will come alive too.

Watch Your Words

Christian educator, Ray Rozell, has said, "One of the chief hindrances to effective teaching lies in the choice of words which are either unfamiliar to the pupils or which mean different things to various people." (*Talks on Sunday School Teaching* [Grand Rapids: Zondervan Publishing House, 1956], p. 128.) Communication takes place only when words are understood; so watch your words. Try to speak at the pupils' level of comprehension, but do not "talk down" to them. Take time to explain new words or ideas. Use illustrations that clarify issues, not confuse them. Have the students look up new words or phrases in a Bible dictionary or commentary. Try to eliminate some of the "religious jargon" from your teaching vocabulary.

Practice speaking distinctly and clearly. Work at improving your grammar and pronunciation. These faults, and other mannerisms, can at times distract from *what* you are saying to *how* you are saying it.

Watch the tone and volume of your voice. Try to speak in the middle of your voice range. Speak in a conversational manner, but speak loudly enough so that all can hear comfortably and without straining. Vary the rate and rhythm of your speaking. Use a dramatic pause as you would a punctuation mark—to show emphasis, to mark a change of thought, or to announce a firm conclusion. Be natural—speak to your class as you would in personal conversation—with excitement and conviction, with intensity and emotion.

HOW TO EVALUATE

Evaluation is most effective when it includes a number of different approaches.

Take a few minutes each week to *review your class activities*. Things to consider may include: The lesson aim, the lesson plan, student response, use of methods, and so on. Jot down your observations in a small notebook or on 3 x 5 cards. Try to state your overall reaction to the session in a single word such as weak, fair, good, strong. Then note specific areas of strength and weakness in your presentation. Take a closer look at your weaknesses and ask yourself why you did poorly. Was it that you were inadequately prepared? Did you lecture too much? Was the lesson aim unclear? Was the introduction or application activity weak? Were there distractions and interruptions? You may also want to note some things you can do to correct some of these problems in your next session.

Another effective way to analyze your teaching is to use some type of *self-evaluation form*. The whole staff could do this occasionally, or you could do it individually. The national Sunday School Department has sample forms available or you can make up one of your own. A continuum scale of some of the areas discussed in the unit above may look like this:

Self-Rating Scale

Circle the number under each section which indicates your effectiveness in lesson presentation (1-poor, 8-good):

Poise, Confidence, Appearance
1 / 2 / 3 / 4 / 5 / 6 / 7 / 8

Posture, Gestures, Eye Contact
1 / 2 / 3 / 4 / 5 / 6 / 7 / 8

Cheerful, Friendly, Good Listener
1 / 2 / 3 / 4 / 5 / 6 / 7 / 8

Use of Familiar Terms, Grammar, Pronunciation
1 / 2 / 3 / 4 / 5 / 6 / 7 / 8

Tone of Voice, Volume, Rate of Speech
1 / 2 / 3 / 4 / 5 / 6 / 7 / 8

Use a cassette recorder to *record your session*. This technique can give valuable insights into your teaching such as your use of grammar, distractions, the balance between teacher and student activities, and so on. Some teachers may have access to a videotape machine to use in evaluating their teaching. This technique allows you to both hear and see how you are doing.

Another way to evaluate your teaching is to ask your students to rate your presentation. Give each one a *student opinion form* to fill out anonymously. Include questions on teaching skills, use of a variety of methods, preparation, enthusiasm and interest, opportunity for student involvement, classroom environment, speech, poise, tolerance, appearance, relationship with students, and so on. Also include several sentence completions such as: "The thing I like best about this class is . . ." "This class could be improved by . . ." "It would help if our teacher . . ." "In general I think . . ." A sample student opinion sheet is available from the national Sunday School Department.

Many Sunday schools have a worker achievement program which includes *regular weekly reports* from the teaching staff. These, too, can help you evaluate your effectiveness as a teacher as you indicate changes in class enrollment and attendance, absentees and visitors contacted, attendance at staff meetings, and so on.

Use a *class observer* to help you evaluate your teaching. Arrange for one of the general or department officers or a more experienced teacher to visit your class for a Sunday. After the session ask him to discuss his observations with you. It may be a good idea to have the evaluation in writing also so you can refer back to it as you work on improving your efforts. The same observer may be invited back after several weeks to see if you have corrected some of the areas needing improvement. The observer should have a specific list of things to look for in the class session such as those listed above on the student opinion form. A sample observation evaluation form is included in the fourth unit of the *Fundamentals for Sunday School Workers* course, "Mastering the Methods."

But what do you do after you have evaluated your teaching? How do you use what you have learned about yourself?

1. Set some goals. Determine to do something to improve. Make your goals high enough to challenge your best effort but realistic enough to be attainable.

2. Put your goals down in writing. It is not enough just to have an idea in the back of your mind of areas that need improvement. Get them down on paper so you can refer to them periodically and see what progress you are making.

3. Limit your efforts at improvement to a few items at a time. Don't try to change everything about your teaching at once or you will end up discouraged or changing nothing at all.

4. Devise a plan of action. List specific steps to take in making improvements. If your weakness is poor Bible study, then plan to purchase and use several good Bible study helps. If you need to spend more time in preparation, then set up a plan to begin preparing earlier in the week.

10 Part of a Team

The Bible teaches that the Church is a body that depends on the power of the Holy Spirit and the cooperation of all of its members to do its work. At times the Sunday school teacher working alone in his classroom week after week can forget this fact. He can begin to feel very much alone in the world. He can come to think that he is the only one concerned about the spiritual needs of his students, when in fact, there are many others in the church that share in its teaching ministry. Rather than seeing himself as an isolated individual, the Sunday school teacher should see himself as a part of a team of workers who stand ready to assist and support each other in a number of ways. Other members on the team with the Sunday school teacher include the workers in the other programs of the church, the Sunday school administrative staff, other members of the teaching team, and the leadership of the home.

THE TOTAL CHURCH TEACHING TEAM

The Sunday school is considered by most as the major teaching arm of the church, but there are many other programs that share in that teaching ministry. It is important that Sunday school teachers be familiar with these programs as they relate to their age-level. The chart on the next page lists some of these programs.

Each of these activities offers a unique ministry and a special emphasis that can complement the teaching of the Sunday school. These programs also provide additional ties

PRESCHOOL	ELEMENTARY
Children's Church	Children's Church
Daisies	Prims
Nursery School	Jr. Missionettes
Vacation Bible	Royal Rangers
School	Buckaroos
Child Care	Neighborhood Bible
Programs	Clubs
	Children's Camps
	Vacation Bible
	School

YOUTH	ADULT
Christ's Ambassadors	Women's Ministries
Bible Quiz	Men's Department
Sr. Missionettes	Couple's Clubs
Trail Blazers &	Home Bible Studies
Trail Rangers	Adult Camps
Campus Groups	
Youth Camps	

to the church. Students who are involved in these activities usually tend to be more faithful and involved in the Sunday school as well.

There are several things the Sunday school teacher can do to work with these agencies:

1. Encourage class members to become involved in these

auxiliary programs. The teacher should know which of his members are attending and try to involve those who are not.

2. Announce the activities of the other programs in the Sunday school. Schedules and announcements could be left in the classroom to be distributed to the students.

3. Reports of other activities such as outings and service projects could be shared sometime during the Sunday school year.

4. Sunday school classes and other programs of the same age-level could occasionally combine for social activities and other outings. In this way, class members who do not belong to the other groups could become acquainted with the leaders and learn about their activities.

5. Arts and crafts of other activities could be displayed in the Sunday school classroom or department area. This, too, would help to build interest in these other programs.

6. Special needs concerning some students could be shared with the leaders of the other programs. In this way both the Sunday school teacher and the program leader can join in praying for and working to meet those needs.

7. Visitation programs of the Sunday school and related activities could be combined to avoid duplication of effort. Those who visit the prospective member or his family could represent both the Sunday school and other church agencies. Personnel for visitation efforts could come from various groups.

THE SUNDAY SCHOOL TEAM

To operate efficiently the Sunday school must function as a team. Each person has a special place of service and each place is important. This truth is borne out in 1 Corinthians 12. Paul says each member has a God-given ministry in the body of Christ, and each is no more or less important than any other member.

It is important that each member of the staff see his position as it relates to the total ministry of the Sunday school. An organizational chart will help visualize this. The teachers are responsible for the teaching/learning experience in the classroom, and the administrative staff serves to support the teachers in this effort. The officers are charged with planning the total program of the Sunday school.

Of course communication among the Sunday school staff members is essential. The officers must make their plans and programs clear to the staff, and the staff should have a voice in responding to those plans. A constant flow of information in both directions is vital. There must be openness of expression and acceptance of one another.

Another important ingredient in teamwork is loyalty. The administrative staff and the teaching staff must faithfully support one another's efforts. The teachers have the right to expect that their officers think and speak well of them, and vice versa. Teachers must be loyal to the students as well, and fulfill their class responsibilities with dedication.

The teachers' relationship with their fellow teachers is also important to the overall ministry of the Sunday school team. There are several vital areas in which the teachers must work in close harmony with each other:

Punctuality

Many churches have a policy that a Sunday school teacher is late if he is not in his classroom at least 15 minutes before the scheduled starting time. This practice has some obvious benefits for the students in that they can be involved in constructive activities from the moment they arrive. But it is also important to the rest of the staff that each teacher be there on time. Students coming into a classroom with no teacher present will often create a disturbance that interferes with what other teachers in the area are trying to do. Other students may be reluctant to enter their classroom if they see a group of students from another class loitering in the halls.

The same principle should hold true for those times when the teacher is absent from his class. If the Sunday school has a policy for arranging for substitute teachers, then follow that policy. If the teacher is personally responsible to secure a replacement, he should do so as early as possible. In either case, the teacher should give the substitute a copy of the curriculum materials and brief him on anything he will need to know. If an unexpected absence occurs, the teacher should contact his supervisor immediately.

Class Schedules

Every teacher wants a degree of independence in scheduling class and department activities. And the needs of the different age-levels call for varying programs. But here again the teacher has more than just his group to think about. There are the other teachers and classes to be concerned with. If one teacher plans a noisy opening activity while an adjacent class is beginning with a time of prayer, they are going to have a problem. Here again is a situation that demands careful coordination and teamwork. The teachers in an adjacent area should meet and try to work out a schedule that will be flexible, yet acceptable to others. An attitude of understanding and cooperation will go a long way toward solving problems in this area.

Sunday school teaching is a big job and requires the cooperation and best efforts of everyone on the staff.

THE TEACHING TEAM

In spite of the support of others on the Sunday school staff, teaching a class can be a lonely experience—unless you are a part of a teaching team. Many Sunday schools are now making wise use of the "team teaching" approach. Of course the term *team teaching* is often applied to many different teaching arrangements—husband-wife teams, teacher-assistant teams, interest center teams, and so on. In its simplest form, *team teaching* is two or more teachers guiding the learning activities of the class. More specifically, it involves a team of teachers working together to present a total teaching/learning situation for the entire Sunday school session.

There are numerous advantages in team teaching for the teacher, the pupils, and the Sunday school in general:

Team teaching provides *teachers* with an opportunity to improve skills through concentration in specialized areas. Team teachers also learn from one another and thus develop new skills. The mutual sharing of ideas makes for better lesson preparation and presentation. And team teaching promotes a feeling of group unity.

Team teaching exposes the *pupils* to different personalities and viewpoints and to a greater variety of teaching methods and approaches. Through team teaching, workers can combine knowledge and skills and together offer more than any one teacher could offer alone. Team teaching also ensures a more balanced lesson presentation. Pupils benefit from more individual attention to their personal needs and interests. Discipline problems are minimized since more workers are available to deal with the situation.

Team teaching holds advantages for the *Sunday school* in general in that it is often easier to recruit workers. Team teaching provides in-service training for new workers as they assist on an experienced team. This approach also helps to minimize the problem of unexpected worker absences as other members of the team fill in for the missing worker. Space, facilities, and equipment can often be more effectively utilized through team teaching.

The teaching team involves a lead teacher and one or more co-teachers. The responsibilities of the lead teacher, who should be an experienced teacher and a capable leader, include calling and presiding at team meetings, directing the work of the team in the classroom, and securing materials, supplies, and equipment for the team. He may also serve as the main storyteller or Bible teacher.

The co-teachers may have a permanent assignment in the class or they may rotate assignments. Some of the different tasks the team members may perform are: introduce the lesson or bring the lesson application; lead in music, art, or drama; direct the handwork or craft time; teach the memory work; keep class records; help maintain discipline; visit absentees and prospects; and lead small-group discussions.

The lead teacher and co-teachers must be able to work together as a team. They must learn to trust each other, to recognize each other's strengths and weaknesses, and to share the loyalties of the class. The teaching team should exemplify the body of Christ with the members edifying one another as they exercise their God-given gifts.

Areas to consider in initiating a team teaching program are groupings, scheduling, facilities and equipment, and planning.

Groupings. Team teaching usually results in somewhat larger classes, although the approach can be used successfully with smaller classes also. The size of the class may vary from 15-30 pupils with a teacher ratio of 6 or 8 to 1. This means one lead teacher and two co-teachers would be needed for a class of 20.

Scheduling. Team teaching activities usually replace the department assembly-classroom arrangement. The schedule consists of *large-group* activities such as the Bible lesson or story, music, and worship, *small-group* activities such as presession, discussion, interest centers, and *individual* activities such as memory work, projects, workbooks, and so on. The key words in scheduling team teaching activities are flexibility and variety.

Facilities and equipment. Larger groupings mean larger classrooms. An area previously used for department activities could easily accommodate a team teaching class in a variety of settings. Partitions or doors may be removed from existing rooms to allow for larger, combined classes. Equipment would include large wall-mounted flannelboards and chalkboards, movable tables and chairs, audiovisual equipment, and so on. Various learning centers would be used.

Planning. Team planning is absolutely essential to a successful team teaching class. Activities must be carefully planned so that each worker knows exactly what everyone else will be doing and what he is to do. The session must be developed as a unit with each part contributing to the success of the whole. A detailed planning session should precede each new unit or quarter of study. The team may also want to meet briefly each week to confirm assignments. Honest evaluation is also a vital part of planning.

It is important that each team member attend all planning sessions—and come prepared by reading all assigned materials beforehand. Each worker should feel free to offer his suggestions and ideas and accept his responsibility of preparing for the class session.

Team teaching is not an excuse for haphazard presentation, but offers another area in which teachers can work together. Each teacher should thoroughly prepare his assignments and have his materials on hand. It is important that each worker stay within the allotted time period scheduled for him and help out whenever and wherever needed throughout the session.

THE TEACHER-PARENT TEAM

Educators, psychologists, sociologists, and others all agree today that the home is the basic unit of society and an important learning community. Children spend more time at home than anywhere else. Parents have a greater influence on their children than anyone else. The home provides an ideal teaching/learning situation. Its loving, intimate, 24-hours-a-day associations are unmatched. In the home children learn by observing, listening, imitating, experimenting, and participating.

Christian educators, too, are recognizing the importance of the home as an integral part of the teaching ministry of the church—some say the most important part. The Bible also stresses the importance of the home and the role of the parents in guiding their children. In Deuteronomy 6:4-7 parents are given explicit commandments regarding their teaching responsibilities in the home.

But in spite of the fact that the church and home have much in common, these two great institutions have not always worked together as closely as they should. At times the church has been guilty of competing with the home for its time and resources. On the other hand, the home has some-times assumed that it is the sole responsibility of the church to provide spiritual training for its members.

The fact is neither institution can do the job by itself. The church needs the home and the home needs the church. The Sunday school alone cannot fulfill the goal of seeing the individual grow toward maturity in Christ. If effective learning is to take place in the lives of the pupils, the Sunday school and the home must cooperate, with the Sunday school playing a supportive role. This means teachers and parents are a team. In fact, one of the most valuable aids a teacher can have is a group of cooperative, enthusiastic parents.

Ways the Sunday School Can Reach the Home

The teacher can never effectively reach the home until he has visited there. It is difficult for the teacher to understand the student until he understands his family environment. A *visit* to the home will reveal the atmosphere in which the pupil lives and determine the forces which complement or compete with the teaching of the Sunday school.

During the visit the teacher should try to observe attitudes and relationships in the home. He may also be able to get a reaction from the parents about the progress of their children and any special problems the parents see in their children's lives.

Letters may also be used to reach the home. At the beginning of each quarter the teacher may send a letter to each student's parents outlining the topic of study for the quarter. The teacher may also suggest ways in which the parents may help the students in lesson preparation and ways to review the lessons such as retelling the story, repeating the memory verse, or using the take-home papers. The teacher may also alert the parents to various articles, books, or magazines they can secure to supplement the lesson study.

An *open house* is another good way to reach the parents. The open house could be conducted on an all-school basis, or each department or division could sponsor the event. The program could feature displays of materials, visual aids or projects, demonstrations of typical class sessions, ways to reinforce the lesson truth at home, and so on. The pastor and other Sunday school leaders should be involved along with the workers and possibly several parents. The program should not be longer than 1 hour in length and should conclude with light refreshments and a time of fellowship so parents can become acquainted with one another and with the Sunday school staff.

Ways the Sunday School Can Minister to the Home

1. *Assist the home in the salvation of its members.* The Sunday school and home share the responsibility for the salvation of their members, but the home often looks to the church for help. The teacher may be in the best position to minister to both the student and his parents. The Sunday school must be concerned about reaching parents as well as children. If the parents can be brought to Christ, they can assist in winning their children. Look for opportunities to minister to unsaved family members when visiting the home. The Sunday school may also consider sponsoring home Bible study groups to reach those who would not attend church. The emphasis in special programs such as Christmas or Easter should also be on reaching unsaved family members who may not attend church any other time. The church may also offer an elective course to train Sunday school members in how to win other members of their family to Christ.

2. *Training parents in family living.* Nearly every occupation requires some form of training and examination before a person is allowed to begin his work. The only exception is parenthood. It is often assumed that parents will come by their needed skills by some intuitive process. Unfortunately this is not always the case. The Sunday school can have a real ministry in preparing parents for and assisting them with their family responsibilities.

This training should include help in determining the Biblical foundations and purpose for the Christian home. Parents need to understand their respective roles and their relationship to each other.

Parents also need help in raising their children. Many young parents, having grown up in a permissive society, need to understand the Biblical principles of child discipline. The church also has a responsibility to train parents to instruct their children in matters of sex education. The Sunday school could offer a series of electives to cover these and other topics.

Many parents need help in administering family finances. The Sunday school can help by providing teaching on Biblical principles of stewardship. Guest speakers from local financial institutions could be invited to share with the parents in the areas of budget, insurance, wills, and so on.

3. *Training children in family living.* Children and youth too need training regarding their place in the family. Larry Christensen says: "God's order for children is compassed in a single command: 'Children, obey your parents in everything for this pleases the Lord.'" *(The Christian Family* [Minneapolis: Bethany Fellowship, 1970], p. 55.) The teacher's task is to implant this principle in the heart and mind of the youngest child and continue to emphasize it until he reaches adulthood.

Children need to be taught to accept their responsibilities in the home. The teacher can help them develop the right attitude toward other members of the family. Teenagers need help in understanding themselves and their parents. The teacher can help them maintain good communications with their parents. The Sunday school could sponsor a teen-parent seminar to deal with problems in these areas. The Sunday school could also help prepare older teens for marriage by providing a study on this subject.

4. *Training in family devotions.* Most families agree that family devotions are important, but not all know how to plan for and conduct a meaningful family worship time. Ways the Sunday school can help are: 1) Offer an elective course for

parents on how to conduct good family devotions. 2) Make available a display of good books and devotional guides to use in family worship. 3) Provide each family with complimentary copies of *God's Word for Today* (a daily devotional guide published by the Gospel Publishing House) and *A Family Affair* (a weekly family-at-home activity guide produced by the national Sunday School Department). 4) Prepare and distribute to parents a list of family devotional ideas such as using art, drama, music, etc. 5) Encourage parents to use unscheduled time for informal worship activities such as singing gospel songs while riding in the car, engaging children in conversation about spiritual things while working together, praying together as a family at church, and so on.

5. *Resources for family life.* The Sunday school could arrange a display of helpful books and magazines on family life. These materials could be made available for purchase or loan. Each family could also be provided with a bibliography of recommended books and periodicals. Any films, filmstrips, or tapes available to the church should also be made accessible to parents.

6. *Family life seminars.* The Sunday school could sponsor various kinds of family conferences, parent-teen seminars, couples retreats, and so on. Family Week, the second week in May, is an ideal time to plan these activities. The Spring *SS Action* magazine includes plans and ideas for Family Week.

7. *Family life program.* The Sunday school should appoint a family life coordinator and a standing committee to direct its ministries to the family. This group could coordinate many of the ideas suggested in this unit. The Assemblies of God Sunday School Guidelines provide help in setting up a family life program.

Ways the Sunday School Can Involve the Family

There are numerous ways the Sunday school can involve the family in the teaching/learning process:

1. The teacher can solicit the help of the parents for various learning projects at home such as research and report assignments, handwork projects, special programs, and so on.

2. Parents can help children with their Scripture memorization work. A letter to the parents could explain what is expected of the children. Hints should also be given to help the parents assist their children in learning the assigned verses.

3. The Sunday school teacher should ask the parents to assist their children in lesson preparation and other assignments. The teacher may suggest a regular time and pattern for lesson preparation.

4. The assistance of the parents is needed in helping the students apply the lesson at home during the week. The teacher may want to send a quarterly or monthly letter to the parents suggesting ways they could interact with the students at home.

5. The Sunday school could promote a family-at-home night and provide suggestions for family activities such as those found in *A Family Affair*. Care should be taken to keep the designated family-at-home night clear on the church calendar.

6. The Sunday school could sponsor various family activities such as a family camping trip, a family sports tournament, family picnics, family service projects such as help for a shut-in, family visitation programs, and so on.

As Dr. Raymond Brock has said: "There is no better way of increasing the effectiveness of Sunday school teaching than by reinforcing it at home during the week. When the teacher enlists the cooperation of parents in extending the influence of the Sunday school beyond a single hour to a week of consistent living, the Christian experience becomes a way of life." *(Sunday School Counselor,* April 1963, p. 5.)

Bibliography

For Further Study

Askew, Sandra K. *A Handbook for Guiding the Preschool Child.* Springfield: Gospel Publishing House, 1976.

Barrett, Ethel. *Storytelling—It's Easy.* Grand Rapids: Zondervan Publishing House, 1960.

Clark, Ronald W. *A Handbook for Guiding the Elementary Child.* Springfield: Gospel Publishing House, 1976

Edge, Findley B. *Teaching for Results.* Nashville: Broadman Press, 1956.

Gangel, Kenneth O. *24 Ways to Improve Your Teaching.* Wheaton: Victor Books, 1974.

Getz, Gene A. *Audiovisual Media in Christian Education.* Chicago: Moody Press, 1972.

Henning, Samuel H. *A Handbook for Guiding Adults.* Springfield: Gospel Publishing House, 1976.

Hurst, D. V., and Dwayne E. Turner. *Mastering the Methods.* Springfield: Gospel Publishing House, 1971.

LeBar, Lois E. *Children in the Bible School.* Westwood, N.J.: Fleming H. Revell, 1952.

Leypoldt, Martha M. *Learning Is Change.* Valley Forge: Judson Press, 1971.

McManus, Ronald F. *A Handbook for Guiding Youth.* Springfield: Gospel Publishing House, 1976.

Richards, Lawrence O. *Creative Bible Teaching.* Chicago: Moody Press, 1971.

Sapp, Phyllis Woodruff. *Creative Teaching in the Church.* Nashville: Broadman Press, 1967.